Noted author Brad Steiger, proposes several theories to explain Third Kind confrontations, including—

Secret Society hypothesis: Perhaps centuries ago a secret society of scientist-alchemists developed an advanced technology, which they have managed to keep hidden in underground or undersea cities. They may be subtly guiding us—or they may be awaiting the appropriate moment to conquer the entire world.

Astronauts from Atlantis hypothesis: The UFOnauts are the descendants of an ancient civilization on Earth, who developed space flight and who return from time to time to visit the home planet.

Extraterrestrial Tricksters hypothesis: Extraterrestrial intelligences are misleading mankind and deliberately confusing us in order to provide a cover for undisclosed activities here on Earth.

UFOnauts examine our soil and atmosphere, carefully observe our behavior, imprison us for biological studies—and may ultimately threaten our very existence!

ALIEN MEETINGS

by

Brad Steiger

ace books
A Division of Charter Communications Inc.
A GROSSET & DUNLAP COMPANY
1120 Avenue of the Americas
New York, New York 10036

ALIEN MEETINGS

An Ace Original

First Ace Printing: January 1978

Published simultaneously in Canada

Printed in U.S.A.

CONTENTS

Introduction   vii

CHAPTER ONE   Close Encounters with
                       Humanoids   1

CHAPTER TWO   They Have Always Been
                       with Us   7

CHAPTER THREE   Establishing Contact with
                       Alien Intelligence   20

CHAPTER FOUR   The Little People:
                       UFOnauts or
                       Leprechauns?   34

CHAPTER FIVE   UFO Repairmen   69

CHAPTER SIX   Robots and Androids   78

CHAPTER SEVEN   The Wretched Uglies   92

CHAPTER EIGHT   The Men-in-Black:
                       UFOlogy's Bad
                       Guys   109

CONTENTS

CHAPTER NINE   UFO Encounters May Be
Hazardous to Your
Health!   125

CHAPTER TEN   Interrupted Journeys and
Cosmic Kidnappers   150

CHAPTER ELEVEN   Angels in Spacesuits   181

Bibliography and Notes   211

INTRODUCTION

In our day of space-age sophistication and instantaneous communications media, the number of reports of men and women who have confronted what appear to be alien beings has increased remarkably. Since the modern age of UFO sightings began in the United States, with Kenneth Arnold's sighting of "flying saucers" near Mount Rainier on June 24, 1947, recent national polls have indicated that as many as twenty million Americans claim to have seen unidentified aerial objects. A significant portion of those who have become a part of the UFO experience have stated that they have observed or encountered alien beings associated with the enigmatic phenomenon that haunts our skies.

Dr. J. Allen Hynek, currently a professor of astronomy at Northwestern University in Evanston, Illinois, served for nearly twenty years as astronomical consultant to the U.S. Air Force on the Project Blue Book study of Unidentified Flying Objects. Dr. Hynek has freely admitted that when he first heard accounts of men and women who claimed encounters with occupants of UFOs, his natural prejudices prompted him to exclude the episodes from his study.

Alleged contacts between humans and humanoids never failed to receive a great deal of notoriety, but they were given exceedingly short shrift by Air Force investigators. And, with but few exceptions among the civilian UFO-research groups, cases involving sightings of UFOnauts were dealt with summarily and with superficial assessments of the mental stability of the witnesses.

Stubbornly, the "little-green-man syndrome" persisted in UFOlogy, and Dr. Hynek, who now directs his own Center for UFO Studies, has conceded that "no scientist should discard data simply because he doesn't like it."

It was in his book *The UFO Experience* (Regnery, 1972; Ballantine Books, 1974) that Dr. Hynek presented his six major classifications of UFO reports:

Nocturnal Lights: colored globes that maneuver about the sky as no conventional aircraft can.

Daylight Discs: metallic appearing objects that can be tracked on radar, give off a humming noise, and move with tremendous speed.

Radar Cases: objects which may be verified by sightings from the ground or by airplane pilots as well as with radar visuals.

Type Four: near approach of a UFO with no physical effects.

Type Five: close encounter with physical evidence.

Type Six: close encounter involving humanoid occupants.

According to Dr. Hynek, Type Six, the close encounters of the third kind, "constitute what is probably the most incredibly bizarre aspect of the UFO enigma."

Dr. Hynek told writer Timothy G. Beckley, for *UFO Report*'s August 1976 issue, that the Center for UFO Studies has an estimated eight hundred sightings of the third kind on file.

Introduction

There seems little question that this "incredibly bizarre aspect of the UFO enigma" holds a great deal of fascination for men and women with even a cursory interest in Unidentified Flying Objects. The contention than an unseen world peopled with beings that can now and again become visible and interact with human-kind has long fascinated our species. Whether such in-telligences be considered angelic, elfin, or extrater-restrial, our global literature, sacred and secular, mysti-cal and mundane, is replete with accounts of *Homo sapiens* encountering beings from other dimensions of reality or from other worlds and other universes. One can debate whether these entities are psycho-logical or physical in origin and whether they can truly exist apart from the human psyches which attest to them, but the accounts of humankind and its involvement with "the Other" are as old as the cave paintings and earliest oral traditions of our species.

In this book, I hope to document not only that Third Kind encounters still occur on a global basis, but that the phenomenon is happening more frequently than ever before. If we are being conditioned for a mass landing of UFOnauts or a program of increased inter-action with the Other, then this book may help us to prepare for such an alien confrontation.

BRAD STEIGER

February 19, 1977

CHAPTER ONE

Close Encounters with Humanoids

At least as long as man has been Man, there have been accounts of another intelligence—manlike in appearance, yet somehow different, seemingly superhuman—that has been interacting with the struggling and evolving species of *Homo sapiens*.

The "Others" have been called Angels, Star People, Shining Ones, and perhaps, on occasion, demons and devils, as well as gods and overlords. Whatever the name applied, the scenario has remained constant throughout the ages and consistent from culture to culture. The mysterious visitors arrive in fiery chariots, mysterious globes of light, strange aerial vehicles. Occasionally they have appeared in blinding flashes of light; at other times they have approached the witnesses to their activities in a tranquil manner, as though they were friendly travelers one might encounter on a lonely road, transiently shared.

At this stage in our investigations one should attempt to avoid any dogmatic assertions as to the exact identity of these mysterious humanoids. But because man appears by nature to be a cataloguer and a labeler, I feel it may be useful to list hypothetical explanations of Third Kind encounters which UFOlogists, psychical researchers, and other explorers of the unknown have offered and which we shall be exploring in the present book. Each reader may soon select his favorite hypothesis, the one theory that seems to make the most sense to him. Or he may come to suspect that two or more hypotheses may be responsible for Third Kind confrontations.

1. *The Extraterrestrial hypothesis:* The entities are astronauts who come from one or more extraterrestrial civilizations. They appear to have had Earth under surveillance for centuries. They have chosen to conduct their activities secretly for some undetermined reason.

2. *Military Secret hypothesis:* The UFO occupants are actually terrestrial astronauts conducting secret military maneuvers with classified aerial vehicles. This hypothesis could only apply to those sightings in which the UFOnauts look exactly like *Homo sapiens*.

3. *Secret Society hypothesis:* Perhaps centuries ago a secret society of scientist-alchemists developed an advanced technology, which they have managed to keep hidden in underground or undersea cities. They may be subtly guiding us—or they may be awaiting the appropriate moment to conquer the entire world.

4. *Programmed Deceit and Delusion hypothesis:* Both the UFOs and their occupants are something similar to holographic projections or elaborate special effects created by some unknown agency (hypotheses 2 and 3) for some ulterior and as-yet-undetermined motive.

5. *Unknown Terrestrial Life hypothesis:* The UFOs may actually be unrecognized life forms indigenous to the upper reaches of Earth's atmosphere. They may be plasmic, electrical, nearly pure energy forms which have the ability to assume a variety of guises.

6. *Astronauts from Atlantis hypothesis:* The UFO-nauts are the descendants of an ancient civilization on Earth, who developed space flight and who return from time to time to visit the home planet.

7. *Time Traveler hypothesis:* The UFOnauts are our descendants from the future, studying mankind by using the past as a living historical museum.

8. *Other Dimensions hypothesis:* The UFO entities come not from some other physical planet but from an adjacent space-time continuum, actually coexisting on Earth with us, but on another vibrational level.

9. *Planetary Poltergeist hypothesis:* The UFO occupants may be the result of some as-yet-unknown physical law that can at times activate (or be activated by) the unconscious mind. This law—or energy—might not itself be intelligent, but it would be able to absorb, reflect, and imitate human intelligence.

10. *Protean-Psychoid hypothesis:* According to writer Michael Talbot: "They [UFOs] are 'protean' because they are all part of the same chameleonlike phenomenon that changes to reflect the belief structures of the time. They are 'psychoid' in that they are a paraphysical phenomenon and are related to the psychological state of the observer."

11. *Psychic Need hypothesis:* Jerome Clark and

Loren Coleman suggest: "Certain of mankind's psychic needs tap psychokinetic and other psi energies and fashion fairies, apparitions of the Virgin Mary, and UFOs—archetypes which we can experience only as images and symbols. The forms they assume are ancient in the sense that they always have been intrinsic parts of the psyche, modern in that we perceive them in the context of ideas the conscious mind has acquired."

12. *UFOnauts as Archetypes hypothesis:* Both UFOs and their occupants may be quasi-real objects manufactured by the human "collective unconscious." Author John White views Jungian archetypes as "energetic thought fields" accessible through "dreams, meditation, and other altered states of consciousness." He theorizes that there may be "larger, previously unrecognized dimensions of physical events" in which highly evolved entities exist on a grander, paraphysical scale and "influence and guide human affairs."

13. *Extraterestrial Tricksters hypothesis:* Extraterrestrial intelligences are misleading mankind and deliberately confusing us in order to provide a cover for undisclosed activities here on Earth.

14. *Magic Theater hypothesis:* UFO manifestations are the result of the "magical" machinations of elves, "wee people," and other paraphysical entities who have coexisted with mankind as companion species and appear to participate somehow with *Homo sapiens* in an evolutionary design.

15. *Supernatural hypothesis:* The UFOnauts are the same entities as the angels which are described by so many religions as the messengers of God. They remain

concerned about the inhabitants of Earth as part of their mission of guidance and/or salvation.

16. *Reality Game hypothesis:* The UFOnauts are playing a teaching game with mankind, in which our concept of reality is being gradually changed. In the teasing fashion of a Zen riddle or a Sufi joke, we are being provoked into higher consciousness.

In my *Gods of Aquarius: UFOs and the Transformation of Man* (Harcourt Brace Jovanovich, 1976), I have carefully stated my conclusion, based on twenty years of research, that throughout history some external intelligence has been interacting with mankind in an effort to learn more about us or in an effort to communicate to our species certain basic truths. I also note my conviction that a subtle symbiotic relationship exists between mankind and the UFO intelligences. I believe that, in a way which we have yet to determine, they need us as much as we need them.

Although I prefer the hypothesis that the UFO intelligences may be our neighbors right around the corner in another space-time continuum, it is quite possible that either or both species might once have had an extraterrestrial origin. Whatever our respective nativities, I feel that the very biological and spiritual evolution of Earth depends upon the establishment of balance between us and our cosmic cousins.

The format of the present work affords me the opportunity to deal with the objective, physical appearances of the Other in Third Kind encounters with percipients whose testimonies appear to indicate contact with an intelligence external to their own.

Although the intellectual climate is becoming more hospitable to the UFO enigma and public acceptance has perhaps never been higher, there are still those who will consider accounts of contacts between humans and humanoids as tales of fancy, reports of hallucinations, or pernicious attempts to hoax. Dr. Hynek may have explained as well as anyone why even serious researchers tend automatically to look down upon the humanoid cases:

Maybe this involves an atavistic fear of the unknown or of rivalry with another species.

There is, upon closer scrutiny, another factor which I find difficult to sort out. It is odd that the creatures seen coming from these craft should resemble our own *Homo sapiens* race so closely. It is also peculiar that they would be able to adjust to our gravitational pull or breathe our air so easily.

This could only mean that they are mechanical creatures—robots—or they originate from a habitat whose environment is very similar to ours here on Earth.

Perhaps, then, as I suggest in *Gods of Aquarius,* it is not *us* and *them,* it is *we.*

In the final analysis, of course, each reader must resolve the question raised by these encounters with aliens with his own construct of reality. For any thoughtful man or woman, the questions raised by these confrontations with the Third Kind are profound in content and prolific in implication.

CHAPTER TWO

They Have Always
Been with Us

I received a report early in the summer of 1971 from a nurse who was employed at a large hospital in Iowa City, Iowa. She was driving to work one morning at dawn when she saw what appeared to be a cage suspended from a line leading into the sky.

As she drew nearer the object, she found that she could see quite distinctly the figure of a man dressed in a shining, form-fitting suit. The man appeared to be gazing intently at the ground below him, although the woman emphasized that he was too high for her to make out his features.

This particular witness had never had any interest in the paranormal or in UFOlogy, and she stated that in fact she had ridiculed the subject. Now, however, as a percipient, she excitedly spoke of her sighting to both the hospital staff and certain of the patients. A frank woman who speaks her mind, the witness soon told her son-in-law, a member of the Iowa City police force, about her sighting. Eventually the incident was reported in confidence to one of my correspondents, who followed through with an immediate investigation.

My correspondent, Glen McWane, was able to learn that a newspaper delivery boy had also sighted the UFOnaut dangling from the sky at about the same time. Further pursuit of the matter produced a laundry delivery man who had also glimpsed the stranger in the sky.

There was a consensus among the percipients that the being inside the dangling object was thick-chested. His arms and legs were also proportionately thicker than those of conventional *Homo sapiens*.

No one saw the details of the being's face, but the witnesses seemed to agree that it was darker than his shiny suit.

The being was in a cagelike apparatus, enclosed with what appeared to be vertical bars. The cage itself was egg-shaped. The being did move inside, and the woman observer had the definite feeling that he was looking down at her.

Through the police it was learned that a few other formal reports of a UFO had been made on that morning, and that extensive efforts were made to identify precisely what the percipients had seen. Checks were made with local airports regarding any helicopters that might have been in the area. Predawn flyers were suggested as possible culprits. All leads drew a blank.

If modern men and women are confused over UFO-nauts seemingly supported by "skyhooks," one can imagine the interpretation that more primitive folks would have given such sightings. A hovering disc, even *without* a sky-walking entity, might easily have inspired the ancient Egyptians to exclaim that they were seeing the "eye of Horus" looking down on them. The primitive Scandinavians knew that Odin, father of the gods, had only one eye—and there it was, glowing with a god's wisdom and peering searchingly down on them!

Mankind has always believed in an invisible world

peopled by unseen creatures. The Bible supports such a belief and informs us at length that spiritual (non-material) intelligences do exist—and in close proximity to our material world.

In both the Old and the New Testaments we are told that these unseen intelligences are divided into two vast hosts: one, obedient to God and active in good ministries for man, called angels; the other, intent on annoying and harming man and loyal to Satan, called demons.

Such a division may remind us of Edgar Cayce's concept of the primal warfare on Atlantis between the beneficent Children of the Law of One and the evil Sons of Belial. Belial, by the way, is Hebrew for "person of baseness," and is used to designate the prince of devils, Satan.

The term "angel," as used in Scripture, is used to designate an office, rather than to describe a person. An angel simply is a messenger, one who is sent to accomplish whatever mission is assigned to him. Any student of the Bible can readily testify that angels are referred to as actual beings and not simply impersonal influences. Angels ate with Abraham, were lusted after by the Sodomites, grasped Lot by the hand. They refuse to be worshipped by man, but they never turn down hospitality. The manna of Israel was "angel's food," the "bread of the mighty."

Angels stand in relation to God, the Supreme Being, as courtiers to a king. They are not gods, but are themselves created beings, as subject to God's will as are men.

And men do not become angels when they die. The angelic ranks were formed long before man was scooped from the dust of Earth, according to Biblical tradition.

Although angels are frequently called spirits, it is

often implied in the Bible that they have corporeal bodies, but dwell on a higher plane of existence than man. Luke 20:36 states that in the Resurrection the redeemed will be "equal unto the angels." In other words, man shall be raised to the conditions common to those beings who now enjoy certain metaphysical advantages.

When seen on Earth, angels have always appeared youthful, physically attractive, commanding, and they are described in much the same manner as UFO contactees of today describe their "Space Brothers." Even though angels may be mistaken for ordinary men when judged by their appearance alone, those who have confronted them have often felt the physical effects of their majesty. Their appearance is often sudden and accompanied by a bright light. Saul of Tarsus and the guards about Jesus' tomb were blinded by the light of the angels.

One touch of an angel's hand crippled Jacob. The single stroke of an angel's staff consumed Gideon's offering. Zacharias was deafened by an angel's word. Daniel's men fell to quaking at an angel's voice, and the shepherds were overawed by the angelic aerial display that heralded the birth of Jesus. Whenever angels are mentioned, they are described as strong, swift, splendid, subtle as the wind, elastic as the light. No distance wearies them, and no barriers hinder them. An angel entered the fiery furnace to keep Shadrach, Meshach, and Abednego cool, and another entered the lion's den with Daniel and closed fast the jaws of the beasts. The angels of old and the more recently encountered Space Brothers seem to share similar superhuman characteristics.

From the Creation, the angels have manifested an active interest in the affairs of *Homo sapiens*. Job 38:7 tells us how the "sons of God" shouted aloud when the Lord laid the Earth's foundations, settled its dimensions, and set its supporting pillars in place. Moses received the Sinaitic law from the mouths of angels (Galatians 3:19), and the Psalms (103:20, 104:4) tell us how angels have control of nature's laws.

Throughout the Scriptures one caution is given man concerning angels: He is not to worship them. John, the author of Revelation, seeks to worship the angel who has shown him a vision of heaven. He is stayed in this action by the angel, who says, "See thou do it not: I am thy fellow servant, and of thy brethren . . ." (19:10). Although they are quite willing and able to aid man in his crises, angels consistently emphasize that they are *brothers* to man, not his gods.

W. Raymond Drake, author and scholar, believes that numerous classical writers have bequeathed us literary evidence of the visitations of superbeings from other worlds. In an analysis of the works of fifty writers of antiquity, Drake found references to such celestial phenomena as airborne lights, shields, fiery globes, strange ships, and warriorlike "men." In addition, there are mentions of two or more "moons," two or more "suns," new "stars," falling lights, unknown voices, "gods" descending to earth, and "men" ascending to the sky.

Our theologians dismiss the ancient Gods as anthropomorphisms of natural forces, as if entire races for hundreds of years would base their daily lives on lightning and thunderbolts! [Drake once wrote for *Fate* magazine.] Yet logic suggests that the old Gods of Egypt, Greece, Rome, Scandinavia, and Mexico were not disembodied spirits or anthropomorphic symbolisms but actual spacemen from the skies. It seems that after the great catastrophes remembered in legends, the "Gods" withdrew and henceforth have been content merely to survey the Earth, except for an occasional intervention in human affairs.

Among the hundreds of references which Drake discovered and declared to be evidence of extraterrestrial contact are the following:

There in the stillness of the night both consuls are said to have been visited by the same apparition, a man of greater than human stature, and more majestic. [Livy, *History,* Book VIII, Ch. 11, *circa* 325 B.C.]

At Hadria an altar was seen in the sky and about it the forms of men in white clothes. [Livy, *History,* Book XXI, Ch. 62, *circa* 214 B.C.]

Three suns shone at the same time. That night several stars glided across the sky at Lanuvium. [Julius Obsequens, *Prodigiorum Libellus,* Ch. 66, *circa* 175 B.C.]

For before sunset there appeared in the air over the whole country chariots and armed troops coursing through the clouds and surrounding the cities. [Josephus, *Jewish War*, Book CXI, *circa* A.D. 70]

In Rome, moreover, a "Spirit" having the appearance of a man led an ass up to the Capitol and afterwards to the palace . . . Upon being arrested for this and sent by Matermianus to Antoninus, he said, "I go as you bid, but I shall face not this emperor but another." And when he reached Capua he vanished. [Dio Cassius, *Roman History,* A.D. 217]

In Drake's opinion, both the Old and New Testaments are filled with references to extraterrestrial beings communing with man. "Yet," he comments, "they are so intermingled with religious dogmas that present-day thought precludes any dispassionate evaluation of Biblical events."

The researcher reminds us that the Roman hero Romulus was borne to heaven by a whirlwind, that his successor, Numa Pompilius, employed magic weapons, that the classical writers Livy, Pliny the Elder, and Julius Obsequens refer often to mysterious voices, celestial trumpets, and men in white garments hovering in airships or descending to Earth. "By some strange twist of the human mind," he muses, "we worship prodigies in old Palestine as manifestations of the Lord, yet scoff at identical phenomena occurring at the same time only a few hundred miles away."

In A.D. 840, Agobard, Archbishop of Lyons, wrote of witnessing the execution of three men and one woman who had been captured when they left "ships that had come from the clouds." The strangers had been apprehended as they were trading for food with local peasants. Church officials kept the aliens in chains for three days before they allowed the populace to stone them as demons.

In *Otio Imperialia,* Book One, Chapter Eighteen, Gervase of Tilbury writes of an aerial ship which caught its "anchor" in a pile of stones near the city of Bristol around A.D. 1207. When an occupant emerged from the ship to free it, he found himself immediately surrounded by curious citizens. Although the visitor accomplished his task, he seemed suddenly to become asphyxiated by the atmosphere and fell, dying and gasping, to the ground. According to Gervase of Tilbury, the anchor, which the "sky sailor" had cut free before he died, was wrought into "that iron grille for

13

the doors of the basilica which stand open for the public to look at."

A similar incident is recorded in the *King's Mirror*, a book of Old Norse etiquette and general knowledge which dates back to the thirteenth century. A translation of the episode by Albert B. Helland appeared in the March 1958 issue of *Fate:*

There happened something in Cloena Borough which will also seem marvelous. In this town there is a church dedicated to St. Keranius. One Sunday while the population was at church hearing mass, an anchor was dropped from the sky as if thrown from a ship, for a rope was attached to it, and one of the flukes of the anchor became caught in the arch above the door.

The people all rushed out of the church and marveled as their eyes followed the rope upward. They saw a ship with men aboard floating before the anchor cable, and they saw a man leap overboard and dive down to the anchor as if to release it . . . When he came down to the anchor he tried to loosen it, but the people rushed up and seized him.

The Bishop was present when this occurred and forbade his people to hold the man, for he said it might prove fatal as when one is held under water. As soon as the man was released he hurried up to the ship; when he was up, the crew cut the rope and the ship sailed away out of sight.

It is interesting to note that in none of these incidents were the aliens described as anything other than men. The medieval church officials and populace may have placed a certain interpretation on their actions which would correspond to man's own technology at that period in history, but in no instance was the sighted "sky sailor" described as being grotesque or different from the Earthmen in appearance.

During the ten-month period between November of 1896 and September of 1897, metallic, cigar-shaped aerial vehicles were sighted throughout the United States. For those readers who may not at once recall our Earthly aeronautical time schedule, Orville and Wilbur Wright did not accomplish the first successful, man-carrying, powered airplane flight until December 1903, and that initial voyage was barely a hop, skip, and a jump, less than a hundred feet.

Speaking in reference to the UFO flap of 1896–97, Charles Harvard Gibbs-Smith, aeronautical historian for the Victoria and Albert Museum in London, has said with certainty that the only airborne vehicles carrying passengers which could possibly have been seen anywhere in North America in 1897 would have been free-flying spherical balloons. "It is highly unlikely for these to have been mistaken for anything else," Gibbs-Smith commented. "No form of dirigible or heavier-than-air flying machine was flying—*could* fly—then."

Yet not only were the airships seen by hundreds of respectable, sober citizens, but a good many individuals of high repute claimed to have spoken with the aviators of the mysterious craft while the objects rested on the ground.

On April 15, 1897, Adolph Winkle and John Hulle, two farmhands from Springfield, Illinois, saw a grounded airship in a field two miles north of town. The three occupants, two men and a woman, told the farmhands that they stopped to repair their electrical equipment. Passing themselves off as terrestrial inventors, the UFO occupants said that they would make a full report of their airship to the government just as soon as Cuba had been declared free. Since the

Spanish-American War was then in the making, the two farmhands must have written the UFOnauts off as eccentric but highly principled scientists.

On April 21, John Barclay of Rockland, Texas, was startled to see an airship settle down in a pasture adjacent to his house. He welcomed one of the occupants with a Winchester rifle when the man approached his house. Barclay was asked to put down his rifle, as the aviators intended no harm.

"Call me Smith," the UFOnaut said. "I need some lubricating oil and a couple of cold chisels, if you can get them, and some bluestone. I suppose the sawmill hard by has the two former articles, and the telegraph operator has the bluestone. Here is a ten-dollar bill; take it and get us these articles, and keep the change for your troubles."

Barclay was curious. He wanted to see the airship. The Texan was told that the strangers could not permit his examination of the craft. He was pacified, however, when the occupant told him that someday they would return and take him on a trip to repay him for his kindness if he would go quickly and secure the articles which they needed.

Just before the UFOnauts left, the spokesman answered Barclay's persistent questions as to their origin by brusquely stating that they came "from anywhere" and would be in Greece the next day.

That same day, a former senator from Harrisburg, Arkansas, was given an extensive explanation of the airship and its origin after he came upon a crewman hauling water from his well at 1:00 A.M. According to the mysterious aviator, he had gained the secret of suspending the laws of gravity from his uncle. For seven years, the UFOnaut claimed, he had labored to build the airship and to fly it successfully. Now, after a visit to the planet Mars, he would place it on public exhibition.

Frank Nichols, a prominent farmer who lived about two miles east of Houston, Texas, also surprised midnight visitors quenching their thirst at his well. The UFOnauts invited Nichols to accompany them to their aircraft.

One of the crew proudly informed the farmer that they had solved the problem of aerial navigation. The craft was constructed of a newly discovered material that had the property of "self-sustenance in the air," and the motive power was said to be "highly condensed electricity."

According to the voluble aviator, five of the airships had been built at a small town in Iowa. Soon, however, the secret invention would be given to the public. At that very moment an immense stock company was being formed, and within a year the machines were sure to be in general use.

In each instance the UFOnauts quite obviously lied to the contactees who had happened on them and their temporarily grounded airships. Whoever they might have been, the mysterious aviators were not terrestrial inventors. Whoever they might have been, the UFOnauts knew that the term "inventor" was more palatable than "angel" to the average North American materialist circa 1897.

From 1947 to 1970, however, when man had long since accomplished heavier-than-air flight and was looking toward the stars, the term "spaceman" would meet with greater acceptance than "inventor." The post-World War II percipient who was distressed about nuclear bombs, radioactive fallout, excessive population, and unbearable pollution was ready once again to look to the skies for succor, and it would surely be most advantageous for the UFOnauts to assume the guise of a space traveler.

The majority of the serious students of the UFO mystery agree, at least arbitrarily, on three basic kinds of contactee reports.

First, there are the cases in which a UFO occupant is seen briefly by a witness, but no attempt is made at any kind of communication; second, the instances in which a witness sights an occupant and engages in a minimal verbal or visual exchange; third, the "Space Brother" type of confrontation, in which the witness receives lengthy philosophical discourses and elaborate promises of guidance from benign, physically attractive entities.

Although the general public and an overwhelming majority of the practitioners of orthodox science may reject all three classifications of contact experience as complete crackpottedness, the UFOlogists feel that there is enough documented evidence for them to accept a good many of the first-category cases as valid, albeit bizarre, experiences. The second variety of contact, that of limited communication, perhaps, accompanied by a physical examination or a brief tour on board the spacecraft, is, as might be expected, deemed less acceptable to the majority of UFOlogists. The Space Brother category of alleged alien confrontation is almost completely rejected by all but a small percentage of UFO researchers and writers as either intentional or unintentional hoaxes.

"There may be some [contactee claims] which, if more fully investigated, might very well prove true," observed Jerome Clark, a UFOlogist who has spent a great deal of time wrestling with the enigma of contact. "Unfortunately, these stories lack the necessary details to be adequately corroborated; but if they are not spurious, they could prove to be the long-awaited breakthrough leading to the solution of the UFO mystery itself."

In his article "The Meaning of Contact" (*British Flying Saucer Review,* September–October 1965), Clark states his opinion that the UFO occupants want to perform their operations in secrecy and that they go to great lengths to mislead human witnesses who may accidentally observe any of their actions.

Since the beings who pilot the UFOs do not want us to know the true nature of their mission on Earth, Clark argues, they may be using the contactees as a tool with a twofold purpose: "to discourage legitimate inquiry into the saucer field by making it look ridiculous, and to instill false ideas into the minds of those who do go on to investigate the subject."

It is Clark's contention that the UFOnauts have been imparting patently phony information concerning "their identity, their origin, and their purpose" to the contactees. What might the true designs of the UFOnauts be? Clark doubts the theory that they are invaders, although he must honestly admit, along with the majority of UFOlogists, that "exactly why this [contact] is done, we do not know; but it is *being* done, quite obviously."

CHAPTER THREE

Establishing Contact with Alien Intelligence

In 1974 a mind-boggling announcement was made by British astronomer Duncan Lunan, who said that he had deciphered a message that had been sent to Earth from another solar system. Lunan did not release his story to the more sensational elements of the press. He made his claim in *Space Flight,* the journal of the prestigious British Interplanetary Society.

According to Lunan, an unmanned "probe" robot satellite, which was placed in orbit around our moon between thirteen thousand and fifteen thousand years ago, has been transmitting the message at intermittent periods since the 1920s. The satellite was placed near us by dwellers of a planet which orbits a star called Upsilon Boötes, in another solar system. Lunan translated the message as follows:

> Start here. Our home is Upsilon Boötes, which is a double star. We live on the sixth planet of seven, counting outward from the sun, which is the larger of the two.

Our sixth planet has one moon. Our fourth planet has three. Our first and third planets each have one.

Our probe is in the position of Arcturus, known in our maps.

The executive secretary of the Interplanetary Society, Leonard Carter, said that Upsilon Boötes is about 103 million light-years from Earth. The robot probe referred to in the message is only about 170,000 miles from Earth, near the moon, and was placed in orbit about 11,000 B.C. As is fairly commonly known, radio echoes have been received since the 1920s, but they cannot be explained as having originated on Earth.

According to Carter: "Lunan plotted the echoes on a graph. Oddly, they seemed to make up a series of dots outlining the known constellations. But they were slightly distorted. However, Lunan has gone into the question of this distortion and alteration. And the dots related to the constellations as they were about 13,000 years ago."

Duncan Lunan's claims have met with the reserve that one might expect from even open-minded scientists. His report in *Space Flight* indicates that computers on the robot probe transmit the message whenever they are triggered by radio waves sent from Earth at an undetermined frequency.

One of the leading radioastronomers in the United States, Professor Ronald N. Bracewell, said that even though he had reservations about Lunan's interpretation of the signals, he would not discount them altogether. Bracewell advanced a similar theory to explain radio echoes noted in 1927, 1928, and 1934, and he said that he had been exchanging research notes with Lunan for the last few years.

An international conference of distinguished scientists and humanists held at Byurakan in Armenia in the summer of 1971 produced speculations about Earth's interaction with extraterrestrial life that could as well have come from a conference of science-fiction writers:

• Was the origin of our life not on Earth but elsewhere, and was Earth deliberately colonized by intelligent beings from somewhere else? Could we similarly colonize other planets?

• Have we been placed in a kind of zoo or galactic wildlife preserve by more-developed civilizations in the rest of the galaxy?

• Communication with us may be forbidden, so as not to disturb our ecology and foul up the observations being made by behavioral or biological scientists from other worlds.

• A more morbid and grotesque possibility is that we may be in a laboratory situation, being managed by some extraterrestrial beings.

Or, as Charles Fort phrased it, "We may be property."

But how will we ever find out *whose* property we may be if we cannot establish direct contact?

There are certain indications that *someone* has been trying to communicate with us, but we seem to be receiving only fragments of larger messages—or perhaps deliberately and cunningly devised clues to throw us totally off the correct track.

Author John A. Keel has written of the radio signals of undetermined origin which have been flooding our atmosphere since 1899. "Two generations of scientists and astronomers have argued indecisively about their possible meaning and purpose, even though dozens of carefully worded and very explicit messages from some mysterious source have been received all over our muddled little planet," Keel observes. "These messages have been too 'far out' to be accepted by either the scientific establishment or the press. They are allegedly from some alien group in outer space. . . ."

Astronomers, exobiologists, and other scientists have speculated that there are 250 billion stars in our Milky Way galaxy. In addition to that brain-stretching number of stars relatively close to home, these same learned men estimate, there are billions of other galaxies in the universe, each with its own possible 250 billion stars. As many as half of these stars may have planets at what would be the proper distance to allow and sustain biological life forms. To say that there could not be advanced alien civilizations on any number of these millions of planets would be the height of human arrogance.

"It is pure ignorance to assume that Earth is the only inhabited planet in the universe," Charles Gibbs-Smith stated. "Certainly there are other civilizations, perhaps thousands of times older and wiser. And I believe intelligent beings from those civilizations are visiting us in spacecraft—and have been for years."

At the 1966 meeting of the American Astronautical Society in Anaheim, California, a group of leading biologists, geologists, astronomers, and space engineers tried to guard against the tendency toward "temporal provincialism" in a three-day symposium on "The Search For Extraterrestrial Life." The collective opinion of the assembled scientists was that it is most improbable that we are alone in the universe.

Dr. G. J. Wasserburg of the California Institute of Technology told the symposium that "we are all left-overs of products of a long series of nuclear fires." The solar system was formed, said Wasserburg, after a cooking and a mixing which lasted for ten billion years, followed by a sudden freezing.

Dr. Norman H. Horowitz, chief of the bioscience section at the Jet Propulsion Laboratory of the California Institute of Technology, expressed his opinion that life on another planet would not necessarily need to be similar to life on Earth: "All species of animals and plants on Earth are built out of the same kind of organic building blocks—amino acids and nucleotides. Despite appearances, there is only one form of life on Earth. It is theoretically possible for life to develop from building blocks other than those found in our own nucleic acids and proteins. The secret of life lies in the formation encoded in the nucleic acids. These are molecules made up of carbon, hydrogen, nitrogen, oxygen, and phosphorus."

Professor W. T. Williams, a member of the botany department of Southampton University, Southampton, England, delivered a lecture to the British Association for the Advancement of Science stating that "bug-eyed monsters" might truly exist on other planets. To Williams, it is conceivable that there are intelligent creatures swimming in oceans of liquid ammonia on Jupiter, or civilized rocklike beings living on sun-scorched Mercury. As a biologist, Williams said, he is prepared to accept any alien of any shape, provided that he, she, or it is large enough to have a sufficiently big brain.

The Soviet Union has set up an extensive network of radio receivers whose primary purpose is to listen for possible signals from intelligent beings elsewhere in the universe. In October 1973, Samuel Kaplan of Gorki University recorded a series of radio bursts which led to excited speculations that extraterrestrial broadcasts had been received by the radio net.

Scientists at "listening bowls" in the United States were extremely skeptical of the alleged signals from outer-space intelligences. They pointed out that no one in the United States had received the signals. If the broadcast had truly been emanating from a distant civilization, receiving stations all over the world should have been able to pick it up. For another thing, the reported power received was extremely high to have come from a distant source. Although both the Soviet and the American military denied the charge, U.S. scientists blamed a satellite for the "messages from outer space."

But no one has ever known whom to blame for the unidentified broadcast that jumbled astronaut Gordon Cooper's voice transmission during Faith-7.

On May 15, 1963, Cooper was making his fourth pass over Hawaii. At that point, his voice transmission was replaced by someone shouting in an "unintelligible foreign language" on the channel reserved for space-flight personnel. NASA recorded this transmission, but, according to available information, has never been able to identify its source or translate its message.

John Keel states that the most commonly received unidentified radio messages have to do with friendly warnings to stop nuclear testing and to cease hostile and warlike attitudes toward one another. Keel writes:

. . . On August 3, 1958, ham radio operators throughout the U.S. reportedly picked up a strange broadcast on the 75-meter international band. A male voice purporting to be Necoma from the planet Jupiter warned his listeners that the American atomic bomb tests could lead the world to disaster. He spoke for *two and a half hours* in English, German, Norwegian, and his own language which was described as a kind of "musical jibberish."

"It was the most powerful signal ever picked up," one account said. "There was plenty of time during the broadcast for hundreds to listen in, and radio operators called in friends and neighbors and phoned long distance to relatives in other states."

The F.C.C. later denied any knowledge of the broadcast. . . .

James C. G. Walker of Yale University has estimated that if all habitable planets are occupied, the average separation of civilizations is 24 light-years and the estimated length of the search involved to establish contact would take 1,400 years. If only one planet in a thousand is occupied, Walker theorizes, the separation is 240 light-years and the probable length of search would be 14 million years.

It is because of such generation-gobbling periods of time that Walker states his conclusion that our search for extraterrestrial civilizations will, of necessity, be limited to passive listening for signals from a super-civilization that already supports an incredibly advanced technology capable of transmitting a recognition signal throughout the galaxy.

On November 16, 1974, however, the occasion of the dedication of the world's largest radio telescope, at Arecibo, Puerto Rico, inspired the transmission of a deliberate radio message beamed at the stars, the most powerful signal ever sent from Earth. The newly resurfaced radio telescope boasts a 1,000-foot-diameter antenna equipped with a 450,000-watt transmitter. The antenna is able to focus its power to what officials at Arecibo say is the equivalent of twenty-five times all the man-made electricity ever produced on Earth.

The intended listeners for this historic hello are the inhabitants of whatever planets may orbit the estimated 300,000 stars in Messier 13. Scientists selected this particular cluster because potentially it contains enough stars to provide an attentive audience for the big broadcast. Cornell astronomer Carl Sagan speculated that there is "about a 1 in 2 chance of there being a civilization in Messier 13."

Even though the message is the most powerful signal ever transmitted from Earth, it may take 24,000 years for the impulses to be received. As one scientist computed the above data, if there are any of our descendants left on Earth to receive a reply, they will be our great- $\times$ (1.6×10^3) grandchildren.

The communication itself, devised by Frank Drake and staff members of the National Astronomy and Ionosphere Center of Cornell University, is relayed via a radio code composed of binary numbers—numbers written in only two symbols, such as dots and dashes —which can be assembled into a grid 23 characters wide and 73 characters long, totaling 1,679 characters. The key to reconstructing the grid for purposes of translation lies in the fact that 1,679 is the product of two prime numbers (numbers divisible only by themselves and 1). The receiving civilization will have to be advanced enough, of course, to comprehend binary mathematics and prime numbers.

According to *Science News* (November 23, 1974), the message begins "with binary numbers 1 to 10, followed by a series representing the atomic numbers of hydrogen, carbon, nitrogen, oxygen, and phosphorus. Next . . . a series of groups showing the number of atoms in the components of the DNA molecule . . . the first part of a fundamental description of earthly biology. Beneath the DNA ladder is a schematic representation of a double helix, with a binary number down the center showing the approximate number 4 billion (the approximate population of the species) and the number 14 (expressing the height of the pictured earthling as a multiple of the message's 12.6 centimeter wave-length). Next, a schematic of the solar system, followed by one of the Arecibo telescope. . . ."

When scientists consider the reception of radio messages from extraterrestrial civilizations or the prospect of our civilization beaming a signal toward distant stars, they most often consider 1,420 megahertz (MHz) as a natural choice on which to send their communications. For one thing, it is the natural resonant frequency of hydrogen—the most abundant element in the universe—and it is quite likely that both sender and receiver would deduce that the wavelength would eventually occur to the other.

But, as some scientists have pointed out, the very same factor that makes it a good choice (the abundance of hydrogen) also makes 1,420 megahertz a poor one. The transmission must traverse a universe filled with hydrogen-heavy stars that are everywhere blasting out their own natural 1,420-MHz wavelengths, disruptive static to the earnestly beamed message. It is for this reason that Herbert Wischnia, a consulting engineer and the president of Sonitrol/Worcester Corporation, Worcester, Massachusetts, is watching for flashes of ultraviolet laser light, rather than listening for radio signals.

Wischnia reasons that ultraviolet lasers "offer the potential of high power combined with high efficiency." It is this combination, he feels, that makes them "an efficient and logical electromagnetic radiation source which could be used by an extraterrestrial community to announce their presence to us."

Natural static problems would be enormously lessened, according to Wischnia. "Stars with a temperature near that of our sun radiate very little energy in the . . . ultraviolet, so that the telescope receivers are not 'blinded' by natural stellar radiation."

The greatest obstacle to the reception and transmission of laser signals lies in the fact that ultraviolet radiation is readily absorbed by Earth's atmosphere, so that very little actually reaches the surface of the planet. To sidestep this problem, Wischnia suggests that the search be conducted from the Orbiting Astronomical Observatory satellite, utilizing the Princeton University ultraviolet telescope focused on three stars, each about eleven light-years from Earth.

Two of the stars, Epsilon Eridani and Tau Ceti, were the objects of Project Ozma's search for radio signals from extraterrestrial civilizations. In 1960, Ozma listened for several months with the eighty-five-foot radio telescope at Green Bank, West Virginia, as past of the first official attempt to receive possible communications from other worlds. The third star which Wischnia will survey for ultraviolet laser beacons is Epsilon Indi.

In November 1974, the ultraviolet telescope was trained on Epsilon Eridani during fourteen of the Observatory satellite's orbits around Earth. Data are being carefully analyzed for signs of intelligently spaced flashes of ultraviolet laser light. Tau Ceti and Epsilon Indi were scanned during the summer and fall of 1975.

Wischnia, too, is conservative about his time limit for success. "While it is possible to speculate on the success of detecting extraterrestrial laser signals on the very first attempt," he admitted, "it is more realistic to plan for a systematic laser and radio search for the next hundred years."

Such statements are made from the perspective of Earth scientists who are seeking signals from other worlds which will fit their preconceived form of appropriate alien communication. However, is it not possible that Earth has been literally bombarded with bits and pieces of transmitted intelligence from otherworldly sources ever since mankind became enlightened enough to interpret such signals in even a rudimentary fashion?

In the fall of 1956 an engineer at a major electronics firm in Cedar Rapids, Iowa, called my friend

Fay Clark and asked if he might bring over a tape that had been recorded the evening before.

"It appears that they had their scanning device going to see if they could pick up any signals from outer space," Fay recalled for me. "While they were tuned in, a voice started talking that appeared to be emanating from an indeterminate point thousands of miles away from Earth. As I understood the engineer, it would have been impossible for this voice to have come from this planet, but it had talked on for nearly two hours.

"The voice appeared to be sexless. It sounded almost mechanical. The material it was relaying was good, very worthwhile. From time to time it sounded like something one would expect to find in the Upanishad, either poetry or prose that sounded like a cross between Kahlil Gibran and the Bhagavad-Gita . . . what one might term universal truths.

"A few nights later I once again received a call from the electronics firm. The engineer told me the voice was back and said that I should look at approximately two o'clock in the north sky. I saw an object that appeared to be about one third the size of the moon.

"It would move across the horizon, stop, remain stationary for a bit, then drop down a little lower, back up rapidly, and move once again across the horizon. It repeated this back-and-forth process six times before it accelerated speed terrifically fast and moved out of sight.

"The next morning the radio and papers said that the night before an erratic meteor had caused thousands of telephone problems. The Cedar Rapids electronics firm had a track on it, and so did stations in Omaha and Davenport. Apparently, as far as they were able to determine, the 'erratic meteor' was about three thousand miles distant from Earth. What they did not publish, of course, was that the 'erratic meteor' was also a talking metaphysical meteor," Fay said.

The whole affair is reminiscent of the assertion by Duncan Lunan that alien civilizations could long ago have left their own communications satellites near Earth. On the other hand, might it be possible that those same hypothetical aliens established their bases on our own natural satellite aeons ago?

On November 22, 1966, a photograph of the moon taken by the Boeing Lunar Orbiter 2 showed strange spires that had never been seen before. A National Aeronautics and Space Administration spokesman released the information that the 750-foot-by-500-foot area had six protuberances, the largest of which was estimated at between 40 and 75 feet high and about 50 feet wide at its base.

"One looks like the George Washington Monument," said a spokesman for the Jet Propulsion Laboratory. "Some of the smaller ones look like upside-down ice-cream cones. There are small white dots which cast rather lengthy shadows. In one photo frame there is this one very tall pinnacle and four shorter ones. They appear almost like antenna array."

If the strange spires are indeed antenna towers, then this construction constitutes physical evidence that intelligent life has been at work on the surface of the moon.

Whatever such anomalies eventually prove to be, the question that intrigues most of us is, when undeniable communication is established with alien life forms or when a face-to-face confrontation occurs in our attempt to contact other civilizations, just what will be the physical appearance of our cosmic cousins?

Will they look very much as we do, because we

share a common ancestor who seeded our worlds millennia ago?

Will they be of some other recognizable yet different order of life? For example, what would make better space travelers than a species of reptile? They would be able to maintain lower cabin temperatures and put themselves in the biological limbo of hibernation—possibly for thousands of years.

Will they be evolved to the point where they are almost totally pure intelligent energy, with perhaps, say, a simple silicon skeletal framework? In other words, might they appear to us to be blobs of shimmering light?

Scientists generally agree that intelligent life probably conforms to several givens:

First of all, the creature must breathe air.

Second, the being probably would not be much larger than the largest human, and might very well be smaller. The square-cube law applies a limiting factor: If you double the height of a being and maintain the same proportions for the rest of the body, the weight will increase at least eight times.

An intelligent being would have to weigh at least forty pounds, according to theoretical rules of biological construction. The brain of any advanced intelligent being must have a high mental capacity, and must weigh at least two pounds. This allows us to estimate the minimum possible size of the alien. Assuming that it is based on a biology similar to our own, the smallest-sized intelligent alien would be as large as, say, a Chow Chow.

The basic rules of biological construction eliminate three-eyed aliens with five ears.

Two eyes are most logical. One eye would not enable the being to estimate distance and would limit side vision. Two eyes combine to enable three-dimensional perception. Additional eyes would only confuse the impulses reaching the brain.

Two ears can afford proper awareness of the direction of the sound impression, as well as an approximation of the distance from which it emanates. More ears would only scramble the messages reaching the brain.

It would also be necessary that the eyes and ears be situated in the being's skull, as near as possible to the brain, so that the time lag between the reception of danger signals and the appropriate muscular reaction is as short as possible.

The spaceman must have some form of legs and feet. A pair of hands with bending fingers and thumbs enables the most efficient use of tools. No appendage other than a hand will suffice for this purpose. A claw or beak or talon will not suffice. Nor would a tentacle, since it can only pull, not push.

The ubiquitous sightings of UFOs and their sometime attendant "humanoid" occupants may well afford us our first clues—if not our first physical evidence— in establishing contact with extraterrestrial life.

Many UFO researchers stoutly maintain that an unidentified *someone* keeps almost continually busy charting our planet. Other UFOlogists insist that messages are being sent and contacts are being made with members of our species.

The UFO alarmist sees such activity as the methodical preparations of an alien race plotting the total enslavement or annihilation of Earth's population.

Other UFO investigators suggest that the UFO intelligences may be concerned about assisting us through a coming time of great purification. UFO skeptics scowl and ask why *any* superintelligent species would bother with our beleagured and battered mud ball in space.

CHAPTER FOUR

The Little People:
UFOnauts or Leprechauns?

It is interesting that a number of those who have confronted occupants of UFOs have commented on the fact that the entities spoke in a language that sounded like Chinese. Many other percipients have said that while the entities spoke in English (or whatever the percipient's native tongue), they used a singsong speech pattern. Others have maintained that the occupants actually seemed to be singing to them.

On July 17, 1967, a group of young French children left the village of Arc-sous-Cicon shortly after 3:00 P.M. to go for a walk through fields dotted with bushes. They had been walking upward along a gentle slope leading to a pine forest when one of the little girls who had been in the lead began to sob, and ran back toward her home as quickly as her legs would carry her. She told her mother that she had surprised several "little Chinamen" who had been sitting behind a bramble bush and that one of them had gotten to his feet with the apparent intention of grabbing her.

A few moments later, two teenage girls claimed to have seen a strange little entity with a protuberant belly running from bush to bush. The creature wore a short jacket and appeared to move distinctly faster than a human being. The girls also heard the entities speaking in a "strange singsong fashion."

Forty-year-old Rosa Lotti (née Dainelli) lived on a farm in a wooded area near Cennina, a village near Bucine in the Italian province of Arezzo. On November 1, 1954, the mother of four had a solitary encounter with two tiny entities who emerged from a small craft.

It was 6:30 A.M., and Rosa carried a bunch of carnations to present at the altar of Madonna Pellegrina. As she entered a clearing, she saw a barrel-shaped object that immediately attracted her curiosity. It looked to her like a "spindle," barely more than six feet in length. It looked like two bells joined together, and it was covered by a metallic material that appeared more like leather.

Two beings suddenly emerged from behind the craft. They were "almost like men, but the size of children." They wore friendly expressions on their faces and were dressed in one-piece gray coveralls that covered their entire bodies, including their feet. Their outfits also included short cloaks and doublets, which were fastened to their collars with little star-shaped buttons. Helmets crowned their small but "normal" faces.

The little men were vigorous and animated, and they spoke rapidly in a tongue that sounded to Rosa very much like Chinese. There were words like "liu," "lai," "loi," and "lau." They had "magnificent eyes" full of intelligence. Their features were, in Rosa's testimony, "normal," but according to her recent appraisal, she said that their upper lips seemed slightly curled in the center, so that they appeared always to be smiling. Their teeth, although big and broad, seemed to have been filed down and were somewhat protuberant. To a countrywoman such as Rosa, their mouths appeared "rabbitlike."

The older-looking of the two beings continually laughed like one of Santa's merry elves, and seemed concerned about making contact with her. He startled her, however, when he snatched away her carnations and one of the black stockings she was carrying. The surprised Rosa remonstrated with him as best she could despite her timidity, and the being gave her back two flowers before he wrapped the others in the stocking and threw the bundle into the spindle.

As if in exchange for the stocking and the carnations, the little men stepped away from Rosa to fetch two packages from inside the vehicle. Before they could return with their exchange gifts, Rosa took advantage of the moment to escape. The frightened woman ran through the woods for several seconds. When she at last turned to look back at the entities, they and their strange craft had disappeared.

Rosa told her story to the village *carabinieri,* her priest, and others who knew the woman to be "absolutely free of any sort of foolish fancifulness or empty reveries."

Eighteen years later, an Italian UFO study group revisited Rosa Lotti and secured a number of fresh details in what has become a classic UFO encounter of the Third Kind.

Writing in *Flying Saucer Review,*[1]* Sergio Conti stated that Rosa wanted to emphasize that she had not felt fear when confronted by the entities. Alarm had come later, after she had fled the scene. She had begun to run when the older of the two beings produced a package that she felt was a camera. For some reason, she did not want her picture taken by them.

Conti comments that the presence of the humanoids seemed to create a state of tranquility in Rosa, a

* See Bibliography and Notes for all citations.

manifestation consistent with other contact reports. It appears as though atavistic fears manifest themselves only after the percipient has begun to consider the unknown phenomenon from a distance. Psychological disturbances are seldom felt by the percipients while they remain with the "visitors."

Many reports of confrontations with entities from UFOs seem to follow the pattern mentioned by Conti. When a craft lands and beings emerge, the viewer generally becomes panic-stricken and may even enter a state of shock. But when the being comes close to the percipient, the witness often experiences a state of tranquility, especially while communicating either tele-pathically or verbally with the UFOnaut. When the being returns to its craft, the percipient lapses back into his or her former state of fear.

Such a pattern of fear-tranquility-fear has led to the conjecture that the UFO entities are able to transmit tranquility to the percipient only when in close range. Perhaps it is a feeling that exudes from the entity's aural body, rather than a telepathically transmitted message. Many a contactee has fled the scene on seeing a craft land—even though hearing his name being called by the UFOnauts—without ever having experienced the peace that might have come.

Rosa Lotti described the vehicle in a flurry of minute details that show how significant she deems the experience nearly two decades later:

"In the thickened part of the spindle, it had two portholes, on opposite sides to each other, and in the center, between them, there was a little door, enabling me to see inside. I saw two little kiddie chairs set back to back, each of them facing toward one of the port-holes."

Rosa now denies that the entities' lips were curled back. She feels that the cleanshaven beings had mouths that were perfectly "normal." Nor did the craft spook-ishly disappear after she had run about a hundred meters. Rosa insists that it was the press reports that had the craft and the entities vanishing so mysteriously. The little men and their spindle were still there when she at last paused to look back.

Conti writes that there is now a "vast network of collateral eyewitness accounts" available—from per-cipients ranging from stonemasons to students, from workmen to court employees—to provide validation of the Cennina phenomenon that is "well nigh irrefutable." All of these accounts confirm that the "spindle" came down over the thicket at Cennina at about 6:30 A.M.

CONTACT WITH ALIENS ON RÉUNION

The island of Réunion is located in the Indian Ocean, between Mauritius and Madagascar. It was there, on July 31, 1968, that a sighting of a UFO was made at nine o'clock in the morning. UFOs are sighted all over the world, at all hours of the day, and during all seasons of the year, but this report included some-thing extra.

A thirty-one-year-old farmer by the name of M. Luce Fontaine testified that he was in the middle of a small clearing in an acacia-tree forest, where he had been picking grass for his rabbits. Suddenly he noticed an oval object in the clearing, about eighty feet from him. It appeared to be suspended in the air at about twelve to fifteen feet above the ground. The outer edge of what he described as a "cabin" was dark blue, while the center part appeared to be lighter and more transparent, like a screen. Above and below the object had two shiny metal feet.

Fontaine, who is married to a teacher and has children, is considered hard-working and completely honest. With those credentials established, let us go on to include Fontaine's statement that in the center of the cabin he saw two individuals with their backs turned to him. The one on the right then turned around to face him. Fontaine estimated his height as about ninety centimeters, or roughly three feet. He was dressed in a one-piece, overall-type uniform and a helmet.

"Then both turned their backs to me, and there was a flash, as strong as the electric arc of a welding machine," Fontaine added. "Everything went white around me. A powerful heat was given off, and then as if there were a blast of wind, a few seconds later there was nothing there any more." [2]

After the object disappeared, Fontaine went to the area where it had been, but he was not able to find any marks or indentations in the ground. An absence of physical evidence is not too surprising, since he had noticed the UFO hovering at about twelve to fifteen feet above the ground.

Fontaine next told his wife what had happened, then the police. "And everyone at once believed me," he commented to the reporter from *Lumières dans la Nuit,* a French journal that interviewed him.

The next day the formal inquiry began, conducted by Captain Maljean of the St.-Pierre constabulary and Captain Legros of the Service de la Protection Civile, who went directly to the site. When devices to detect radioactivity were employed, their findings showed a reasonable amount of radioactivity in the area, as well as on the clothing that was worn by Fontaine the day of the sighting. According to Legros, there were eight radioactive spots, on pebbles and tufts of grass, reading up to sixty thousandths of a roentgen—quite low, but possibly indicating that "something" had been there. One explanation for the low roentgen count was the fact that the actual readings were not taken until about ten days after the alleged landings, and there had been heavy rains during that period.

There were other sightings of UFOs in the area, including one over the neighboring island of Mauritius on August 11. That craft was described as cigar-shaped, and it was also seen from Réunion.

For those who dogmatically believe that UFOs can only be solid "nuts and bolts" metallic craft, the suggestion that a craft could simply disappear is preposterous. However, reports of rapidly materializing and dematerializing UFOs are filed so frequently that we must entertain the possibility of other than conventionally material objects.

If the object acquired its energy from some source as yet unknown to us, it might suffuse the UFO with a glow while the craft is changing velocity in order to hover or depart. The glow emitted might be similar to ultraviolet or other invisible rays and render the object invisible to our vision apparatus.

Another theory that may explain the now-you-see-it-now-you-don't phenomenon is that the UFO uses a spacetime continuum as a channel of transportation, enabling it to bypass lengthy travel over vast distances.

ENCOUNTER ON A SKI SLOPE

Ever since man began to report his strange encounters with humanoid beings, he has spoken of being immobilized by a bright light. For the past four decades we have been bombarded with science fiction stories, Buck Rogers and Flash Gordon serials, and futuristic films depicting heroes and villains utilizing "ray guns" that stun, kill, or even disintegrate their victims. Only recently has our science invented the laser beam, a light capable of destroying.

The more advanced our own technology becomes, the more the old accounts of confrontations with strange beings gain credence. Reports that once seemed preposterous now make us ponder just how so many contactees and percipients over the centuries could have described implements and artifacts which are only now coming into being and utilization.

A reporter for a Swedish magazine was sent to Finland to investigate the story of a humanoid sighting that reportedly took place during the late afternoon of January 7, 1970, in a forest near the village of Imjarvi in southern Finland.

The two witnesses, Esko Viljo, a farmer in his late thirties, and Aarno Heinonen, a thirty-six-year-old forester, had been skiing. Both men were characterized as athletic nondrinkers.

They had paused in a glade on that cold afternoon. After about five minutes, they heard a buzzing sound and saw what they described as a very strong light in the sky. The buzzing gained in intensity, but the light halted in its flight pattern.

Suddenly the light seemed to be surrounded by a cloud that gave the appearance of a reddish-gray mist, pulsating with a strange light. Puffs of smoke began pouring from the top of the cloud. The two astonished men watched in complete silence.

The cloud then descended to about forty-five hundred feet, allowing the skiers to see inside. They saw what they described as a round, metallic object, roughly nine feet in diameter. On the bottom side of the strange object, which was flattened, they saw three hemispheres and a central tube.

The object hung in the air for a time, and the buzzing continued. The buzzing increased in intensity and the mist disappeared as the object descended slowly. When the UFO was about nine to twelve feet above ground level, it stopped, as did the buzzing.

"It was so close," Heinonen commented, "I could have touched it with my ski-stick." [3]

A light beam was suddenly emitted from the tube. After moving around for a bit, the beam stopped, making a brightly illuminated circle on the snow. The beam, the two men agreed, was about three feet in diameter. The two remained perfectly still as a red-gray mist descended over the area.

"Suddenly," Heinonen reported, "I felt as if somebody had seized my waist from behind me and pulled me backward!"

He recalled stepping back about a foot. "And in the same second, I caught sight of the creature. It was standing in the light beam with a black box in its hands." Heinonen said that the box had a round opening and emitted a pulsating yellow light.

"The creature was about ninety centimeters tall with very thin arms and legs. Its face was pale like wax. I didn't notice any eyes, but the nose was very strange. It was a hook rather than a nose."

He continued his description by stating that the ears were very small and narrowed toward the head. The creature wore overalls of a light-green material, boots of a darker green, and white gauntlets that reached above its elbows. Its fingers were bent like claws around the black box.

Viljo then added his comments regarding the strange humanoid: "The creature stood in the bright light and was luminous like phosphorus, but its face was very pale. Its shoulders were thin and slanting, with arms like those of a child. I did not think of the clothes, only noticing that they were greenish in color."

Viljo also described the creature as short, less than a meter tall, and quite thin.

As the two men stood there watching the creature, it turned a bit and placed the opening of the box in front of Heinonen. The pulsating light was very bright, almost blinding. Then, as the creature continued to stand in the light beam, the thick red-gray mist swirled from the object and large sparks came from the illuminated circle above the snow.

The men reported that the sparks were large—about three feet in length—and were red, green, and purple. When the sparks hit the two men, they did not feel them. The mist then became so thick that they could no longer see each other, the light beam, or the creature —which by this time they had observed for a total of about fifteen to twenty seconds.

Throughout the experience, the men did not become alarmed and did not talk to each other.

Viljo continued the report: "Suddenly the circle above the snow decreased. The light beam floated upward like a trembling flame and went into the tube of the object. Then it was as if the mist was thrown apart, and above us the air was empty."

About two minutes after the mist dispersed, Heinonen noticed that his right side had become insensitive. When he took a step forward on his ski, he fell to the ground.

"I had my right side toward the light. My right leg hurt, and I could not feel anything from my right foot upward. I could not raise myself, although I tried several times," he said.

He left his skis, and Viljo helped him reach the village and the cottage of Heinonen's parents, where he reported that he did not feel at all well. He had difficulty breathing, a headache, and pains in his back, arms, and legs. He soon vomited, and when, later, he passed water, it was as black as coffee.

That same evening Heinonen consulted a physician, Dr. Pauli Kajanoja, who found his blood pressure much lower than normal, indicating a state of shock. The doctor gave him some sleeping pills.

The symptoms continued. Heinonen's arms and legs continued to be sore, and he also had problems with his balance. Although he felt cold, he did not have a fever.

A third visit to Dr. Kajanoja was made six days later, on January 14. Heinonen was given medication to improve blood circulation, but the symptoms continued, preventing him from working.

In May Heinonen was still complaining of being sick with headaches and with pains in the stomach and the back of his neck. He was still unable to work. He reported that he and Viljo had once returned to the place where they had seen the object and the humanoid, and that he had then become even more ill.

In addition to the physical pains which he had to endure, Heinonen also had periods of loss of memory. He had not eaten well since January. Though he had been in perfect health before the encounter, he now found that even the lightest task caused him to tire.

Viljo did not escape completely unharmed, although he did not feel anything abnormal immediately after the encounter with the creature. However, about an hour later his face became swollen and turned red. He began walking a bit off balance. The next day he found that he too had difficulty with his balance, as well as a light feeling in his legs. His hands and chest became red two days later, and he suffered from a headache for about two more days.

On January 12 Viljo visited a specialist about his swollen eyes. Two days later he went to a physician in Heinola, who gave him medicine for blood circulation. Viljo returned to the same doctor three days later, and the physician could find nothing wrong with him—although Viljo reported that when he took his sauna, his entire body turned scarlet.

Viljo wrote a letter to the reporter from Sweden in May, and said that some other people had visited the site of the visitation and they too had become ill within a few days.

The report of Dr. Kajanoja, who examined both men, stated:

> I think the men have suffered a great shock. Esko Viljo was very red in the face and seemed to be a little swollen. They both seemed to be absent-minded. They talked quickly and incoherently. I could not find anything clinically wrong with Hei-nonen. He did not feel well, but it could have been his stomach reacting to the shock. The symptoms he described are like those after being exposed to radio-activity. Unfortunately, I had no instrument to measure that. As to the black urine, it seems inexplicable. Possibly there could have been blood in it, but that cannot go on for several months. It was impossible to diagnose, therefore I could not prescribe any particular medicine.

When the Swedish reporter, a photographer, and an interpreter, together with Viljo and Heinonen, visited the site in June of that year, the hands of Viljo, Heinonen, and the interpreter turned red. Heinonen had to leave the area due to a headache.

The reporter, in line with his journalistic duties, was able to locate two witnesses who reported seeing a strange, strong light in the sky the afternoon of January 7, at the same time (4:45) as that reported by the two skiers. One of the witnesses was Elna Siitari, a farmer's wife from Paistjarvi, a village about fifteen kilometers away from the site. The other witness, a man from the village of Paaso, ten kilometers away, also verified the time of the event, saying that he had seen a light phenomenon. But neither of these percipients reported contact with UFO entities.

NEW JERSEY SOIL SAMPLERS

It was a rather warm night for January 1975 as George O'Barski, seventy-two, drove home from the small liquor store that he owns and manages.

It was about two o'clock that morning as he moved through North Hudson Park on the New Jersey side of the Hudson River. Then, strangely, his car radio suddenly developed a lot of static.

"I began to notice my radio," O'Barski told Ted Bloecher, an investigator for Mutual UFO Network, "it got scratching in it, and a tinny sound . . . I turned up the volume and got more scratching, you know? The radio stops! There ain't nothing, see?" [4]

The car window was down partway, due to unseasonably warm weather. O'Barski reported that he heard a droning sound, a bit like the noise a refrigerator makes. Then he saw something coming down from the skies: "It was a floating thing."

He described the object as round, about thirty feet in diameter, and six to eight feet high, with a dome on top. The object itself was dark, with several lighted vertical windows around the main part of the body of the craft. Each window was about a foot wide and four feet long; they were spaced about one foot apart. O'Barski said he saw nothing at any of the windows other than illumination, about the intensity of household lighting. He also noticed a lighted strip around the object at the base of the dome.

The object then reportedly moved into the nearby park, parallel to O'Barski's car, and came to rest about one hundred feet from him. At first the object seemed to hover approximately ten feet above the ground; then it settled to about four feet over the grassy area. He was not able to determine whether the object rested on legs or any kind of platform.

A square-lighted opening suddenly appeared, and nine to eleven humanoids scrambled down the steps, "like kids coming down a fire escape."

The occupants were all about three to four feet tall, according to O'Barski, and seemed to be wearing some type of coveralls, "like little kids with snowsuits on." They each had on a helmet that was round and dark, like the coveralls. They also seemed to be wearing gloves.

As the occupants descended the steps, each carried a small, dark bag and a small shovel. Each bag seemed to have a string or handle attached to it.

The small humanoids apparently knew their mission well, for they had no sooner reached the ground then they began digging. They dug rapidly in various locations near the UFO and put the soil samples in their bags.

The whole digging episode lasted less than two minutes; then the small occupants climbed the steps once again, and the craft took off, totally disappearing within twenty seconds.

O'Barski said the occupants did not act like robots

but moved about very much like humans. Although they did not seem to notice him as he watched them, he gradually became frightened.

After the UFO and its occupants left, O'Barski's car radio once again worked normally.

In summing up the report, O'Barski commented, "I've been held up in the [liquor] store lots of times in thirty years by men with pistols and knives. I've been plenty scared, but nothing like this, ever. I was petrified!"

We should consider the thought that Earth may be visited periodically by a variety of extraterrestrial intelligences and may be hosting an assortment of indigenous entities. Some of the beings seem primarily interested in examining our soil, as if they were chemically analyzing it, as we are presently doing with our Mars robot probes. Other entities appear to be concerned only with mankind's spiritual awareness. A third type of being seems to be a casual, almost indifferent, observer, while still another type of entity appears peevish, if not somewhat threatening, to the percipient.

Interestingly, the descriptions of the "soil samplers" consistently describe the same small, elvish beings, three to four feet in height. And such consistency appears to hold with the age-old allegations that the wee people have always been ecologically minded, intensely concerned about the way their human cousins treated the Earth Mother.

Again, we should consider that just as our own culture has its specialists—religionists concerned primarily with one's soul, chemists devoted to the laboratory, meteorologists dedicated to the weather, and so forth—so might another species in another cultural context compartmentalize its interest groups.

THE ROCKVILLE, VIRGINIA, HUMANOIDS

Let us place ourselves in the position of intelligent beings who wish to contact the inhabitants of an alien planet. We could communicate with them through a voice transceiver placed strategically in a town square. Those contacted through the transceiver might then legitimately describe us as square, metallic beings with a screenlike face and wires protruding from our bodies.

If we decided to include a visual image via television, the aliens, supposing they were slightly less technically advanced than we, might relate in awesome terms that we could come and go with the speed of light and that we were capable of invisibility until we willed that our presence be made known. Our actual image, depending upon the size of the television screen, might indicate that even though we possessed godlike powers, we were actually very tiny individuals.

Could it be possible that many of the accounts of "fairies" and "elves" issuing from UFOs actually describe an alien intelligence's image projected for purposes of communicating with a less technically sophisticated species?

At about one forty-five on the morning of May 11, 1969, twenty-year-old Mike Luczkowich, a student at Manakin, Virginia, was returning home after a date with his girl friend in Rockville, Virginia.[5]

Just as he passed the Rockville General Store, Mike noticed something about fifty yards ahead of his car. At first he thought it might be a couple of deer, but he soon realized that he was observing two figures about three and a half to four feet tall. The creatures were wearing spherical helmets that looked as large as basketballs. Circling each helmet was a pale green band that reflected the headlights of the car. The beings were motionless at first, but they soon scurried off and ran up an embankment to the left of the witness.

The first two creatures had barely disappeared when a third small creature appeared from the right side of the road and quickly joined the others by climbing over the embankment.

Luczkowich reported that the men were dressed in light-brown coveralls that were somewhat baggy in the legs but were tight-fitting at the ankles. He did not see any arms, and he could not detect features behind the oversized helmets.

The student was shaken by the experience, and he did not tell anyone of the encounter until Sunday.

On Monday, Luczkowich and three other men returned to the site. They were able to locate a definite trail through the poison ivy and honeysuckle on the embankment the three beings had scaled.

Beyond the embankment they found a barley field with a path through it, such as the three humanoids might have made. After a few feet they noticed two flattened areas, where small entities might have thrown themselves down in the grain field. The crushed barley at one of the impressions, according to Luczkowich, showed the imprint of two small bodies, while another impression outlined one small body.

Investigators from the National Investigative Committee on Aerial Phenomena (NICAP), a civilian group, arrived the next week, but by that time the barley had been mowed, and with it the evidence that might have answered a few more questions. No photographs had been taken at the time the four men noticed the imprints in the barley field.

About a half mile west of the area, and about two hours earlier on that same evening, May 11, eighteen-year-old Debbie Payne had reported seeing an oval-shaped, luminous object over her house as she arrived home from a date. The object appeared rather bright, then dimmed, and became bright twice more before she and her date reached the house. Unfortunately, Miss Payne's escort said that he did not see the object himself, but the proximity of the two sightings may indicate a relationship between the three small humanoids and the UFO over Miss Payne's home.

HIT-AND-RUN IN OHIO

On the stormy night of March 30, 1967, while driving home in southern Ohio, David Morris found himself steering his automobile into a nightmare that will haunt him forever. It was about 2:30 A.M., and Morris had just topped a hill crest when he saw a glowing cone-shaped object twenty-five to thirty yards off to the left side of the road.

Morris slowed to thirty miles per hour and stared in disbelief at the mysterious vehicle in the wheat field. The craft was about twenty-five feet high and approximately twelve feet wide at its base.

Suddenly Morris's attention was brought back to the highway. Running across the road into the glare of his headlights were four, possibly five, figures in some kind of orange uniform.

Morris braked his car, but he was unable to stop. There was a sickening thump as the right front of his auto struck one of the "men." The automobile slid eight to ten feet on the rain-slick highway before it came to a halt. Morris reached for the door handle. His first impulse was to help.

Then, he said, the thought flashed through his mind: "If I killed one of them, they will kill me!" He pressed the accelerator and left the scene.

Later, a civilian UFO investigator stated: "All investigation seems to indicate that David Morris is telling the truth. For at least a week prior to his encounter we were receiving reports almost nightly of orange-colored lights of various shapes and sizes. After Morris's encounter, this type of sighting shut off abruptly! Now we have been receiving reports of red-colored lights again almost nightly . . . I am wondering how all this will end."

STRANGERS AT THE SIDE OF THE ROAD

It was about 10:45 EST on March 20, 1967, when a man—pseudonymously dubbed "Mr. Rible" by Robert A. Schmidt, then secretary of the Pittsburgh UFO Research Institute—asked his daughter Jean to accompany him in the family Volkswagen to the outskirts of Butler, Pennsylvania, in the hope of glimpsing some unusual aerial light phenomena that he had been observing. Since they lived only a mile from a private airfield, Rible felt rather strongly about his ability to distinguish conventional from unconventional lights in the sky.

They parked the Volkswagen on a back road and after a few minutes' wait spotted two globes of light. The illuminated objects appeared at first to be two airplanes flying parallel to the highway, toying with the notion of landing on the road. A short time later they gave the appearance of having done just that. Then, from a distance of about a quarter of a mile away, the vehicles came up the slope toward the Ribles at a speed of about eighty miles per hour. The Ribles, who had stepped out of their automobile for a better look at the globes of light, now prepared themselves for what seemed to be an inevitable collision with the two berserk aircraft.

The crash never came, but the Ribles were confronted with an impact to their construct of reality that challenged them—and all of us.

The lights seemed to transmogrify into a semicircle of five figures, who stood just a few yards from the hood of the Ribles' Volkswagen. Both Ribles jumped back into the car, but while her father worried over starting the vehicle, Jean got a good look at the humanoids. Schmidt quotes her as describing them in the following manner:

". . . They looked like human beings, but their faces were totally devoid of expression . . . Their eyes, if you could call them such, were horizontal slits . . . I could not see any irises or pupils—just slits. Their noses were narrow and pointed, not unlike a human nose, and their mouths were slits like the eyes." [6]

Jean said that four of the figures were about five feet seven inches in height, while the fifth was about five feet tall. They all wore a kind of flat-topped cap, with blond hair showing to ear length. The shorter humanoid had hair to the shoulders, which caused Jean to suspect that it might be a woman.

All five of the beings were dressed alike, in sloppy gray-green shirts and trousers. The skin on their faces and hands was rough-looking, resembling "scar tissue or skin which has been severely burned."

Jean admitted that the semicircle of staring entities gave them "the creeps."

"We heard no noise in connection with either the lights or the figures," she told investigators. When the engine was started, the Ribles had to "reverse and then go forward and 'round the figures to miss them."

Under persistent questioning designed to ferret out details of the experience that might have been forgotten under stress, Jean remembered what may have been a most significant factor. As the lights swiftly approached their car, she heard a "chorus of voices" in her head, not with her ears. She seemed to have sensed them with her brain.

"The voices said: 'Don't move . . . don't move . . . don't move . . .' They kept repeating 'Don't move . . . don't move,' but they dragged it out—'Dooooooo-nnnn'tttt Mooooove.' When the lights vanished, the voices stopped at once," Jean said. "My father didn't hear a thing and so I thought I was hearing things—but now I'm not too sure."

HUMANOID IN A BELGIAN GARDEN

UFO sightings have been taking place worldwide constantly since 1947, but for some reason humanoid sightings have been rare in Belgium until quite recently. One of these recent visitations was witnessed by a twenty-eight-year-old Belgian, who is identified simply as V.M. and who is said to live in the industrial city of Vilvorde, just a few miles northeast of Brussels.[7]

A very strong wind blew over the area on that particular night in December 1973. V.M. awoke at about 2:00 A.M. to go to the toilet, which is located in a small courtyard next to the kitchen of his duplex. He tried to be quiet so as to not wake his wife, and he took a flashlight so he would not have to turn on the bedroom light.

Just as he got to the kitchen he heard a noise outside the house that sounded like a shovel falling. He then noticed a greenish light filtering into the kitchen. As he looked out the window he saw what he described as a glow that reminded him of the diffused illumination of an aquarium. His garden was usually in complete darkness at that hour.

He continued to watch the garden area from which the greenish light issued, and soon saw a small being dressed in a glowing uniform that was the source of the light. The humanoid seemed to have normal arms and legs and was of about average build. The uniform looked as though it had been coated with a metallic paint, and the creature's head was covered by a bowl-shaped transparent helmet with a hose leading down to a rectangular backpack that covered his back from waist to shoulders.

The clothing, so far as V.M. could see, had no buttons, zippers, or seams. Around the alien's waist was a belt that emitted a red light from a square box where a buckle would normally be.

The humanoid was in the garden, and he was operating a device that looked like a vacuum cleaner or a mine detector. He moved the object back and forth over a pile of leaves V.M. had left in the garden.

The little being seemed to have difficulty walking. He swayed from side to side, and he bent his knees slightly as he walked.

Suddenly V.M. turned his flashlight on the garden area, and the humanoid turned around. Apparently he was not able to turn his head, because he moved his entire body. It was then that V.M. could see that the strange little visitor had a dark complexion. V.M. could make out neither a nose nor a mouth, but he clearly saw small pointed ears and yellow, oval-shaped eyes. The humanoid's eyes were huge and shiny and circled at their edges in green. The pupils were also oval and black.

The strange little visitor looked at V.M. face to face. Then, with the detector in one hand, he raised his other palm and made a "V" by spreading the index and middle fingers.

With that sign, the little humanoid walked over to the garden wall and proceeded to walk right up one side, like a housefly, and down the opposite side.

In a few moments an aura of white light appeared on the other side of the garden wall. A sound was heard above the breeze as a circular object climbed a short distance into the air. The object hovered for several minutes, making a noise like a cricket.

V.M. described the upper portion of the UFO as phosphorescent orange, topped by a transparent dome, which emitted a greenish light. The lower half of the craft was claret red, and three lights could be seen in the lower portion, one blue, one red, and one yellow.

An insignia was visible on the platform that ringed the UFO, and V.M. described it as a black circle crossed diagonally by a yellow flash that resembled a lightning bolt.

In a short time the UFO rose vertically into the air, then shot skyward, leaving a glowing trail behind it. Soon it was nothing more than a speck in the wintry sky.

V.M. did not receive any verbal or telepathic messages from the humanoid, nor did he experience fear. He also told investigators that he did not feel the least bit upset by the whole event; in fact, he soon went back to bed and slept soundly for the rest of the night.

The next morning V.M. made a check of the garden, but he was not able to find a single trace of the humanoid in the form of tracks or depressions in the ground. So far as he could tell, nothing had been disturbed by the nocturnal visitor.

THE VEGETABLE MAN

It was a beautiful summer day in July 1968. Jennings Frederick had been hunting woodchuck with a bow and arrow, but he had bagged nothing by sundown and headed for home. He was deep in thought when suddenly he heard what he described as "a high-pitched jabbering, much like that of a recording running at exaggerated speed."

According to writer Gray Barker, the voice seemed to be saying "You need not fear me. I wish to communicate. I come as a friend. We know of you all. I come in peace. I wish medical assistance. I need your help!" [8]

But who, what, was giving this message? And did Frederick hear it externally or pick it up through telepathy?

Suddenly, there it was, a being with semihuman facial features, long ears, and yellow, slanted eyes. Its arms were no bigger around than a quarter, and they terminated in hands that had three 7-inch-long fingers with needlelike tips and suction cups. Its body resembled the stalk of a plant in shape and color, for it was slender and green.

At first Jennings thought his hand had become entangled in a briar patch, but he soon realized that the humanoid had gripped his hand and was drawing blood from it. Suddenly the creature's eyes turned from yellow to red and seemed to rotate as spinning orange circles. Jennings's pain immediately stopped as the hypnotic effect of the eyes caused him to freeze in his tracks.

The requested medical assistance, in the form of a transfusion, seemed to last only about a minute, after which the creature released him and ran up a hill, covering more than twenty-five feet with each step.

The pain returned to Jennings's arm, and he headed for home. Shortly he heard a humming sound that made him think that the Vegetable Man might be taking off in his flying saucer, or whatever craft he had arrived in.

Jennings returned home, but he decided that, rather than face ridicule, he would tell his family that he had been scratched by a briar. The story did not come out until he related it to his friend Barker some months later.

UFOs were not strangers to Jennings Frederick and his family. His mother had had an experience when Jennings was still in school.

After getting her husband off to work and the children ready for school, she washed the breakfast dishes. She glanced out the kitchen window and saw what she thought was a child playing in the field near a hillside. She was concerned that the youngster might touch the electrified cattle fence, and she decided to go to the porch to warn the youngster.

When she got there, however, what she saw was not a child, but a small black or dark-green creature. It was stuffing dirt and grass into a small bag it was carrying. Just beyond the creature was a saucer craft, with an elevator extending to the ground. The small creature was attached to the craft by what appeared to be a cable of some type.

The craft was about ten feet in diameter and five feet high, cream-and-silver-colored, with rows of windows under the dome. The machine seemed to rotate in a clockwise direction, while emitting a humming sound.

The little humanoid appeared to be more animal than human. It was naked, and had pointed ears and a tail—all of which gave it a satanic look. She could detect no facial features.

Mrs. Frederick ran into the house, jumped into bed, and covered her head with the blanket, hoping that whatever it was would disappear. A few minutes later she looked out the window, just in time to see the creature enter the craft and take off. The humming got louder as the craft rose into the air "as light as a feather."

Mrs. Frederick told no one of the event until her son, Jennings, came home from school. A UFO buff, he knew what evidence to look for and immediately went to the area of the landing.

He found a depression in the ground where the stem of the craft had rested, and from the description of the craft and the soil consistency he estimated its weight at at least a ton. He also found clawlike tracks, from which he determined that the creature weighed about forty-five pounds. Jennings sent hair specimens in the depressions, together with plaster-of-Paris impressions of the tracks, to the Air Force. Such evidence convinced Jennings that his mother had actually seen what she said she saw, and that she had not been dreaming.

According to Gray Barker, the Air Force offered "an inane explanation—a weather balloon—and never returned the physical evidence."

Jennings Frederick's encounters with UFOs and related subjects did not end with the Vegetable Man, although they did take a brief respite during his tenure in the Air Force. After his discharge he was living with his parents once again, and one morning between one and four o'clock he was awakened by a flash of red light.

He instinctively drew his .38 service revolver from under his pillow and started to investigate. He thought at first that the source might be the gas furnace, but he soon noticed a small canister about the size of an apple bouncing around the living-room floor. Suddenly a hand grabbed him, and he felt the prick of a needle in his left arm.

He was confronted by three men dressed in black turtleneck sweaters and dark slacks, with ski masks on their faces. One of them said, "The dogs have been darted and everybody gassed!"

"What about this one?" another asked.

"He's going out soon—he's half asleep," came the reply. "Don't worry about the needle. It will make his arm sore for a day or two, that's all."

Just as the canister was about to reach Jennings, the men put on gas masks, and the last thing he remembered was seeing one of the men put the canister in his pocket.

The men, according to Jennings, pulled something over his face and began asking him questions about UFOs and what he thought they actually were. They also asked what time it was and what he thought of the future. At that point Jennings apparently passed out, for he remembers nothing more until the next morning, when no one else in the house reported anything strange from the previous night. He assumed that fumes from the canister had "put them out."

Gray Barker theorized about his interview with Jennings Frederick: "Maybe he was one of *them*. Maybe he had interviewed me, instead of me interviewing him."

He soon dismissed this idea, however, as he drove

home through the rolling West Virginia countryside, and settled for the idea that Jennings was a man possessed, not by insanity, not by Christian devils, but by the UFO enigma.

THE HIDDEN ONES: PUCK AND
THE WEE PEOPLE

In 1962, some enterprising men in a small village in Iceland decided to enlarge a herring-processing plant. According to Icelandic tradition, no landowner must fail to reserve a small plot of his property for the mysterious "Hidden Folk," and a few of the rural people pointed out to the men that any extension of the plant would encroach on the plot of ground that had been set aside for the Little People.

The businessmen laughed. They possessed modern, nearly unbreakable drills, plenty of dynamite to supplement the tirelessly gnawing teeth of the drill bits, and a top-notch crew of highly qualified men to operate the equipment. Progress would not be held up by ridiculous superstitions.

But the bits of the "unbreakable" drill shattered, one after another. An old farmer came forward to repeat the warning that they were trespassing on land that belonged to the Hidden Folk. The workmen, secure in their education and enlightenment, laughed at the aged man and expressed their smug shock that such a doddering, superstitious old fool could still exist in modern, jet-age Iceland.

But the drill bits kept breaking.

Finally the manager of the plant, although professing disbelief in such prattle, agreed to the old farmer's suggestion that he consult a local seer to establish contact with the Hidden Folk of the area and try to make peace with them. In a trance, the seer told the manager that there was one particularly powerful entity who had selected that plot as his dwelling place.

The Hidden One was not unreasonable, however. After the seer had explained that the businessmen really needed the extra space, the entity agreed to find another place to live. The Hidden One asked only for some time to make his arrangements. If the manager would delay the drilling for five days, the entity would have enough time to find another plot of ground.

The manager felt a bit weird bargaining with something he could not even see, but he took note of the broken drill bits and told the seer that the Hidden One had a deal. When five days had passed, the workmen resumed drilling. From then on the work went efficiently, and not another bit was broken on the "unbreakable" drill.

Admittedly, such tales sound as if they came from a time much earlier than our own, but whatever strange powers the Little People exerted over their human neighbors in centuries past seem to be just as potent today. What were, or are, the fairies of legend, folklore, and—dare we say it—fact?

In most traditions, especially in the British Isles and Scandinavia, the fairy folk were supernormal entities who inhabited a magical kingdom beneath the surface of the earth. Fairies have always been considered to be very much akin to men, but they have always been known to be something more than mortal men. The fairies have never been popularly conceived of as belonging solely to the realm of spirit. As many of the ancient texts declare, the fairies are "of a middle nature betwixt Man and Angel." One factor has been consistent in fairy lore: The "middle folk" continually meddle in the affairs of man, sometimes to do him good, sometimes to do him ill.

Some Biblically oriented authorities have sought to cast the fairies in the role of the rebellious angels who were driven out of Heaven during the celestial uprising instigated by Lucifer. These dispossessed angels (or demons, depending on one's point of view) took up new abodes on Earth, materialized in human bodies, and took humans as mates, breeding, of course, a hybrid race of entities "betwixt Man and Angel."

Traditionally, the "fairies"—I'll use a commonly accepted generic—are a race of beings, the counterparts of mankind in appearance but at the same time nonphysical or multidimensional. Although they have many more powers and abilities than feeble *Homo sapiens,* the fairy folk are depicted as strongly dependent on man.

Here is one of those interesting cross-cultural references which I so delight in discovering! *Puckwudjinies* is a common Amerindian word which signifies "little vanishing people." Puck, mind you! Robin Goodfellow. The very personification of the woodland elf. Shakespeare's "sweet Puck," who chuckles about how foolish we mortals be.

From here we go to *Puke,* a generic name for minor spirits in all the Teutonic and Scandinavian dialects. *Puke* is cognate wih the German *Spuk,* a goblin, and the Dutch *Spook,* a ghost. There is also, of course, the Irish *pooka* and the Cornish *pixie.* And chop off the suffix of *Puckwudjini* and we are left with *jini,* the Arabs' denizen of magical lamps.

So we have a paradimensional intelligence revealing itself almost universally as Puck. From Amerindian tribes to Nordic tribes to Arabian tribes, we have precisely the same kinds of interaction and the same lessons, the same game play, the same purposes, the same goals.

For centuries various individuals have felt that they have come up with "convincing evidence" that the Little People exist. Call them fairies, brownies, banshees, red ones, the good folk, or leprechauns, or personify them as Puck, Robin Goodfellow, or Mab—persistent tales and an enormous library of folklore have been built around the stories of the Little Folk.

The fairies are said to enchant humans and take advantage of them; it is related that they can marry humans, or cast a spell on a likely lad or lass and have their way with him or her, against the mortal's will; they seem to delight in kidnapping children and adults and whisking them off to the underground fairy kingdom.

On the other side of the coin, it is said that fairies can materialize to help a farmer harvest his crop or help a housemaid clean up a kitchen; that they can guide humans with their ability to divine the future; that they stand by to assist at the birth of a favored child, and tutor and protect him for the rest of his life.

It is interesting to consider that the same things said to be true of the Little People might also be said of the reported instances in which occupants of UFOs have involved themselves with *Homo sapiens*.

The UFOnauts have been reported to hypnotize, or "enchant," men and women in order to make Earthlings more malleable. There have been instances reported in which they had sexual intercourse with Earthlings, in what would appear to be an attempt to create a hybrid. There are numerous documented cases in which it seems that men, women, and children were kidnapped and taken aboard UFOs. And the UFOnauts have been reported working closely with certain representatives of *Homo sapiens* throughout the years, aiding and advising them, and, who knows, maybe in a less-sophisticated time they even helped get in the crops.

Perhaps the most widely known bit of fairy lore is the scene in which a farmer comes upon one or more of the Wee Folk digging in the earth. The farmer naturally surmises that the little one is burying his gold, so he snatches the fairy by the leg and forces him to tell of his treasure. That done, the farmer frees the sprite and marks the spot so that he will be able to find it again with little effort. By the time he returns with his implements, the spot has been altered or confused in some manner to make the excavation of the gold an impossible task.

This tale has been told with endless modifications and variations, but it remains essentially a story of a fairy outwitting an avaricious man. Less widely known are the many stories in which the man who discovers the fairies at their work is whisked away by them to the fairy kingdom, from which he may return much later as an old man who thinks that only a day has gone by—or from which he may never return.

Perhaps the fairies are not digging for gold at all. Perhaps the Little People are UFOnauts taking soil, mineral, and legume samples and do not want their activities known.

Observe how the following account might have been told as a fairy tale if it had happened four hundred years ago.

On August 17, 1962, Rivalino da Silva, a miner from Diamantina, Brazil, came upon two strange people approximately three feet tall engaged in digging a hole. Startled at da Silva's sudden approach, the tiny men ran into the bushes. While the amazed man stood rooted to the spot, a hat-shaped, fiery object ascended into the sky.

Da Silva must have found it difficult to assess the bizarre scene that had just been played out for him. He went home that night, slept on it, probably tried to integrate the whole weird business into his experience. The next day, when he told his friends at the mine what he had seen, they laughed at him.

But shortly after dawn of August 20, his twelve-year-old son, Raimunda, was awakened by strange voices. He swore later that he heard them say "Rivalino is in here. He must be destroyed."

Raimunda saw a shadow of something not quite like a human being, and only half as large, float, rather than walk, through his bedroom.

Then his father began to move as if entranced. He opened the front door and walked toward two large globes that hovered about six feet off the ground. The strange objects hummed, and blinked with an eerie kind of light.

Raimunda screamed at his father to come back, but the man continued to walk toward the mysterious floating objects. Before the boy could make a move to grab his father by the hand and shake him out of his strange trance, the globes had emitted a heavy, yellowish smoke that completely enveloped his father's form.

When the smoke cleared, the floating balls had disappeared—and so had Rivalino da Silva.

Raimunda and his two young brothers, Fatimo and Dirceu, ran to the police station, sobbing out the unbelievable tale of their father's disappearance. The police began an immediate investigation.

At the da Silva home they found a strange, cleanly swept area in the dust about 16 feet in diameter. They could find no sign of any footprints or tracks in the area. The officers did find a few drops of blood about 160 feet from the house, but even though laboratory analysis established the fact that the blood had come from a human, there was no way to determine whether it was da Silva's.

Police tried to break Raimunda's story and began to operate on the premise that the boy had murdered his father and had somehow hit on an ingenious method of disposing of the corpse. But they were soon convinced that the terrified twelve-year-old sincerely mourned his lost father and was psychologically incapable of murder.

Then a fisherman reported that he had seen peculiar globes circling the da Silva home on the evening of August 19. Da Silva's miner friends reported his encounter with the little men. The case was officially closed as "unsolved."

Place this story in a different time and a different cultural context, and you have a fairy tale of a workman who came upon two Little Folk burying their gold. After failing to trick them into giving up their treasure, the man is whisked off to the fairy kingdom in a mysterious golden coach, never to be seen again.

Even the descriptions given by men and women who have observed UFOnauts match those given of the fairy folk. We are not referring to the six-inch-tall creatures with gossamer wings, but to the more common folklore fairy, who stands between three feet and five feet tall, has large eyes, a pointed chin, and rather sharp features.

Almost as common in fairy folklore as confrontations with Little People burying their gold are tales of fairy lovers who seem actively to lust after mortals. Such accounts are beginning to crop up more and more in the annals of UFOlogy. The following is a classic case of the genre:

Antonio Villas Boas, a young farmer who lived near the town of Francisco de Sales in the Brazilian state of Minas Gerais, claimed that on October 15, 1957, he was dragged aboard what appeared to be a machine shaped like a large elongated egg, with three metal spurs in front. His abductors were about his height (approximately five feet four inches tall), and once they had bullied him into the craft they stripped him naked and poked and prodded him with needles and unidentifiable implements.

Then came the real surprise: He was shut into a room with a totally naked woman of the alien species. Antonio described her as having large blue eyes that seemed to slant outward, a straight nose, high cheekbones, a nearly lipless mouth, and a sharply pointed chin. The young woman was truly "hot stuff," because Antonio later came down with the symptoms of radiation poisoning.

Was the female a modern counterpart of the fairy lover? Set this account, which was thoroughly investigated by doctors, in an earlier time, and what would we have? A young farmer, working in his field, is dragged off inside a fairy mound filled with lustrous shining lights, where the fairy queen, who had become enamored of him, makes him her husband. Then, after their honeymoon, when he commits some cloddish human act considered taboo by the fairies, he is once again returned to his farm and his oxen.

Could the romantic tales of dancing fairies and tiny royalty be ancient accounts of UFOnauts as interpreted by the storytellers of long ago in the language of their own time? Could the fairies be elemental entities who have always existed and functioned on Earth, coexisting with *Homo sapiens*, intermingling with him in thousands of subtle ways? A solid kernel of reality may lie at the core of centuries of myth and legend.

CHAPTER FIVE

UFO Repairmen

Just when some UFOlogists have decided that extra-terrestrial godlike beings are visiting us and displaying capabilities which border on the miraculous, we come across accounts in which UFOnaut mechanics are feverishly and *manually* repairing their disabled craft. Such reports cause us to reassess our beliefs and prompt us to attempt to understand more completely just who our visitors might be and why they are here.

In *Gods of Aquarius* I suggested that such devices as apparent mechanical breakdowns might be designed as a sympathetic attention-getting mechanism: "In our day of stalling automobiles, failing washing machines, and fading television tubes, the sight of a sluggish vehicle would indeed gain the immediate attention and sympathy of contemporary witnesses. Once human attention has been attracted, the UFO intelligence could quite easily alter human consciousness. For example, the UFO construct might be symbolically telling the percipient that his *own* technology is breaking down, his *own* culture is in need of immediate repair."

UFONAUTS COME TO CALL

Mr. Jones and the three children had gone to bed for the night. Mrs. Jones was watching *The Tonight Show* with Johnny Carson.

When Mrs. Jones left the TV set and went to the kitchen for a drink of water, she noticed what she thought was a helicopter hovering over the power lines just north of the house and about a quarter of a mile to the east. The object was moving slowly toward the Jones house. Suddenly she realized it was not a helicopter!

She tried to awaken her husband, but the most she could manage was a sleepy reply from him to the effect that she must be dreaming. Mrs. Jones returned to the kitchen. The craft was hovering about twenty to thirty feet from the house.

She then saw "people" inside the craft, one male and two female. The male member of the crew seemed to be staring at Mrs. Jones. So far as she could tell, "Their shape was similar to ours." [1]

The craft itself was said to be shaped like a globe with a platform around it—a description that fits many UFO sightings. The people aboard the craft appeared in silhouette. Mrs. Jones could see no color, but the outlines indicated the sex of the occupants.

Mrs. Jones became frightened as the man stared at her with an almost hypnotic gaze. She looked into his eyes for at least thirty seconds before turning away, but she continued to watch him, fascinated, out of the corner of an eye.

The man, according to Mrs. Jones, was standing in

front of what appeared to be steering controls, and he seemed to be piloting the craft as it moved very slowly.

She continued, without success, her attempt to wake her husband.

One of the women handed the man something—"It was a small object, like a cup of coffee."

The man was very muscular, but all three seemed rather slim and very well built. Their heads and bodies seemed like those of normal human beings to Mrs. Jones. She did not recall noticing whether they had hair, and she never saw their figures below the waist, but she was certain they were ordinary men and women. The craft itself was either white or silver.

Soon the UFO started following the power line, and it disappeared from her view a short while later, at which time she was able to see colored lights to the rear of the craft.

"The little red, blue, and green lights and a vapor trail, or exhaust, of pink, green, blue, and white suddenly went straight up into the air and vanished," Mrs. Jones told investigators.

She also told them that she remained quite restless the rest of that night, while her husband continued his slumbers.

UFO REPAIRMEN IN MONTANA AND NEW YORK

An incident concerning the possible repair of a UFO by its crew was reported by Mrs. Leona Nielson of Walla Walla, Washington.[2]

Mrs. Nielson reported that she and two other women

had gone to their cabin in Montana, near Glacier Park, in February 1970. The three friends stayed up late, chatting and enjoying the beauty of the moonlight as it played on the white snow surrounding the Flat River. The logs in the huge fireplace crackled, a comforting sound for that winter evening of peace and quiet.

It was about one o'clock when the women retired for the night, but Mrs. Nielson was unable to sleep. Suddenly a glow entered her upstairs bedroom, as if from the headlights of a car—but her bedroom window faced the river.

She got up and went outside. She then noticed a long object with a dome and an encircling platform in the lower field. The object was apparently being repaired with some type of welding equipment, as huge sparks were jumping from it, flying across the river and hitting the bank near her cabin.

One of her friends joined her, and the two watched the event for nearly a half-hour, until the sparks suddenly stopped and the strange craft disappeared.

Mrs. Nielson reported that they saw two men running around the platform on the craft. She described them as about five feet eight inches tall, wearing what looked like snowsuits. Their heads were not covered, and they worked and walked as humans would. She estimated that the platform running around the craft was about six feet wide.

The two women watched from their vantage point just inside the doorway of the cabin; the craft was resting in what they estimated was a two-acre area that had been cleared of timber. The craft itself was about fifty feet in diameter.

"My friend and I didn't panic or run. I don't know why," Mrs. Nielson concluded.

A similar incident occurred in upper New York State. November 25, 1964, was the first clear night in a long time in the New Berlin area. For days the skies had been overcast, typical weather for much of this country in late fall, but on this evening the moonlight was beautiful and a generous expanse of stars was visible in the heavens. It was a good night to go outdoors and take in the beauty of the skies, thought Marianne.

She and her husband Richard, a chemical engineer, were visiting their parents during Thanksgiving. Although they lived in Syracuse, the couple had grown up around New Berlin. They were staying at Richard's parents' home, about a mile south of New Berlin. Richard had gone hunting with his father. Marianne was restless and could not get to sleep, so she decided to walk outside for a while.

As she looked to the sky she saw a "shooting star." It made the conventional arc and dropped below the horizon in the east. There was another, but this one did not follow the usual rule for meteorites, which are most common in November. It dropped down in a straight line, near the first one, but then seemed to come down directly over the highway, a bit to the east, near Five Corners. It then followed along the highway. Marianne realized that she was not seeing a shooting star, and that this bright light had an intensity such as she had never seen before—even brighter than a mercury-vapor lamp.

Now she could hear a low hum—a droning sound, "like a water pump running kind of laboriously, and it never changed pitch."

She called her mother-in-law to come out and see whatever it was she was observing in the night sky.

Soon a car passed the corner and drove on down the road. Then a second car showed up, as though its passengers also saw the strange light, and pulled to the side of the road just as the lighted object headed for Marianne. As it did, the car burned rubber getting away from the area, and Marianne, standing on a slight rise in the driveway, made a hasty retreat for the porch, just as her mother-in-law was coming out.

Then the object backed up. Marianne remained within close running distance to the door of the house. At first her mother-in-law wanted Marianne to come back into the house, but then she too decided to stay outdoors and see what the strange object was all about. The UFO eventually came to rest, hovering several hundred feet across the road from the house.

"I felt like I was being observed," Marianne told investigators.[3]

Her dog, an English springer spaniel, was quite devoted to Richard's mother, and it usually made its nightly outdoor trip at about that time. On that night the dog would not leave its mistress's side but stood there shaking and quivering with fright.

A third car came down the road, slowed down as though the driver had seen the object, then drove away at top speed.

The UFO traveled along a creek bed that ran parallel to the highway, moving very slowly, according to Marianne. It then reached the side of a mountain about thirty-eight hundred feet away and settled down on the ridge. Marianne could no longer hear the drone of its engines, but she could still see the bright light.

It was a cold night, and Marianne, persuaded by her mother-in-law, finally went into the house. But she found a pair of binoculars, and continued to watch the object from a window.

Marianne said it was just past one o'clock that morning when she went into the house. The binoculars did not help too much, due to the glare of the light against the lenses. Finally, after tipping the binoculars up and down several times, she was able to get rid of the glare, and she saw what she thought was movement around the craft, caused by what appeared to be men near the UFO.

She was not able to see a definite shape to the object, but she was able to determine that the light was coming from the underside of the UFO, which apparently rested on legs of some sort.

Marianne watched as the manlike creatures carried what seemed to be boxes of tools, two men to each chest. There seemed to be more than one chest, but she was not sure if there were two or three.

She estimated the men to be anywhere from six and a half to eight feet tall, and the legs of the craft at about six to seven feet long. The area of bright light under the craft was estimated at about ten feet in diameter.

Marianne handed the binoculars to her mother-in-law, to see what she could determine about the craft and its inhabitants. According to Richard's mother, the men were five or six in number and were dressed in skin-tight suits, such as those worn by skin divers. The suits were dark, and the men's hands were visible from the wrists, revealing a skin color lighter than the suits they wore. Basically, they looked like men, only taller than average. (Height estimates were based on the height of bushes near the men.)

"They were working on this vehicle like I've seen my father work on farm machinery," Marianne said. "They seemed to have wrenches and screwdrivers and tools such as a man would use to work on a piece of machinery that had gone bad."

Another UFO arrived on the scene and settled down on the ridge near the first object.

From the second craft came another four or five men, who joined those already working on the other vehicle. According to Marianne, they arrived just as the first crew members had removed something that resembled a motor or power supply from the center of the craft. The new crew joined the old in the repair operation.

Marianne said that the men appeared to be cutting a long cable into exact lengths and using the sections for repair of the craft. The men were kneeling, half lying down and leaning on elbows, as they worked. There were ten or twelve in all by now, and some seemed to be bringing things from the vehicle, while others were returning parts to the craft. Marianne commented that she was not able to see the men without the binoculars, but she was able to get a good look at the UFOnauts while using the glasses.

Fear was not absent during the entire event, especially on the part of Marianne's mother-in-law and the dog, which never left the older woman's side. But the two women decided to stay up and to continue their observation of the strange men and their unusual vehicles on the nearby ridge.

"You know," stated Marianne, "if we had called someone they would have come up here with guns and firearms and bothered them. They just wanted to get that thing fixed and get away."

Marianne was convinced that the UFOnauts knew that she did not want to call the authorities, for she was certain that she was being watched, as she was watching them.

The minutes stretched into hours, and it was now 4:30 A.M., according to the kitchen clock. She saw the men lift the "motor" and replace it in the bottom of the craft. But apparently it did not fit properly, so they reversed each step, putting the engine back on the ground and working on it for another ten minutes, before once again attempting to replace it in the craft. Again it would not fit, and the UFOnauts repeated the process—cutting more cable and fitting the sections into place. The replacement failed for a third time, so once again it was removed to the ground level. After a few more minutes of adjustment, however, success was finally theirs!

The men then picked up all of the tools they had been using and returned to their ships.

At 4:55 the vehicle on top of the hill lifted off and disappeared almost instantly. A minute later the second vehicle did the same.

As Marianne commented, "It had been a long night."

Later that day Marianne and her husband decided to walk up to the ridge to see if they could find some concrete evidence of what she had witnessed during the early hours that morning. On arriving at the landing site, they found three places with triangular indentations up to eighteen inches deep. These impressions seemed to indicate that something quite heavy had rested there.

After searching the area for a while, Marianne also found what appeared to be a short length of cable, which she described as tubular, about one inch in diameter, wrapped in a paperlike material. The cable itself was of an aluminumlike metal. Marianne did not think it was actually aluminum, as it did not have the softer qualities of that metal.

When they returned home Richard's mother put the piece of cable away for safekeeping, but when investigators checked out the story, the cable could not be found. Skeptics will suggest that the cable never really existed. Others, who have researched similar UFO cases, will wonder if the cable dematerialized from our physical plane to some other reality.

CHAPTER SIX

Robots and Androids

To answer man's desire for increased leisure, science is going to great lengths to create robots capable of performing distasteful and tedious tasks. It is the current dream of many technologists to fashion economical robots to relieve the housewife of the depressing drudgery of housework; to aid the husband in mowing the lawn and pruning fruit trees; to aid the factory worker in rushing through the apathy of production-line monotony. There is no reason, these futuristically oriented men and women argue, that robots cannot serve mankind in performing mundane chores as well as in sampling Martian soil and probing Jupiter's atmosphere.

Although we might look with caution on entrusting high-level positions of responsibility to robots which might turn traitor, such as "Hal" in Arthur C. Clarke and Stanley Kubrick's film, *2001: A Space Odyssey,* many of us have grown to maturity with complete confidence in such loyal friends as Klaatu in the movie *The Day the Earth Stood Still.* Even from the rather limited perspective of the 1970s, it does not really require a far-forward leap of the imagination to conceive of an advanced alien culture that might find it far easier and more desirable to send their robots to explore and evaluate environments on other worlds than go themselves.

At any rate, it seems that not all UFO occupants are humanoid, for many reports have indicated that the crew of these mysterious vehicles have appeared, in form and demeanor, to be robots rather than men.

One such sighting took place in France at St. Jean-en-Royans on January 9, 1976.

Jean Dolecki was driving his pickup truck on a side road about seven o'clock that evening when he suddenly saw a brilliant ball in the dark night sky. It was Friday night, and Dolecki was hurrying home after a tiring week. He paid little attention to the ball in the sky—at first.

But suddenly the object began to lose altitude, and it appeared to be coming toward him. He slowed his truck down and watched it closely. He studied the object with the care his years as a Baltic seaman had taught him.

"I had the impression that it was a big globe," he told investigators. "It shone as if it were covered with silver paper. I certainly thought it was going to crash onto my truck or right in the middle of the road."

He hit the brakes on his truck hard and pulled over to the right side of the road. He was fascinated by the light of this strange globe. He turned off the ignition, but as he left the truck he decided to leave the lights on to get a better look.

The brilliant globe landed in a field about 340 feet away. He estimated the craft to be 40 to 50 feet in diameter, with the upper part slightly larger than the bottom.

"I don't believe the machine rested on the ground,"

he commented, "because the bottom emitted a bizarre light which did not diffuse around."

Dolecki admitted that he was afraid, and he said that he retreated several feet. He did not get back into his truck, however. Apparently his fascination was stronger than his fear.

Next he saw a door open at the upper part of the sphere; he estimated that it was about six and a half feet high. Three forms, dressed in silvery suits, appeared at the doorway.

"They were not men! I can assure you of that," he emphasized. Rather, according to Dolecki, "They were robots! Giant robots! Of the same height as the door."

Their motions were stiff, with no suppleness, as they rapidly descended from the UFO.

"I saw then that they had small legs, and, for arms, telescopic poles that made me think of fishing rods." He described their heads as "square," but difficult to characterize beyond that.

The three robots moved away from the craft, but only a short distance. They walked like mechanical toys, in jerks and jumps, wagging their arms—or poles—up and down as they moved along.

"I did not move—I could barely breathe! I could only think that the headlights on my truck, which I left on, would surely attract them. But, no, they didn't even notice me," Dolecki said.

About ten minutes passed; then the robots reentered the craft. The door closed and the lights went out, with the exception of those on the very top of the sphere. The machine then took off at a fantastic speed.

"I got back in my truck. Once in the cab, I made the sign of the cross. I was trembling so, I couldn't get started. But there was only one thing I wanted to do—to get home," Dolecki admitted.

When Dolecki finally arrived home, he found that

his wife and daughter had started dinner without him. They could tell by his manner that something was wrong. Dolecki told them the entire story. In spite of their skepticism, he telephoned the local police to make a report of the evening's events.

The police investigator was far less skeptical than Dolecki's family. He no longer made jokes about UFOs. UFOs had been serious business to him since that day in 1974 when two of his men witnessed a mysterious object over St. Nazaire-en-Royans.

To add to the credibility of Dolecki's account was his long-time acquaintance with the investigator, the brigade commander for that region, who knew that he was not prone to hallucinate and that he was a sensible man who would not perpetrate a hoax.

Further investigation of the incident revealed that the reported sighting took place just a short distance from the Alphonse Carrus farm. On that evening, January 9, the Carrus family had been watching television. On several occasions during the evening numbers and letters had flashed across the screen; at other times the picture disappeared. The time of the sighting reported by Dolecki and the time of the Carruses' interrupted television watching coincided. However, another farm family near the site of the incident noticed nothing unusual on their TV screen during that same period of time on January 9.

The investigation of the Dolecki case seems to end here, but there were other similar reports in that region of France—so many, in fact, that local authorities say there were too many to record accurately.

One such case, involving ten-year-old Jean-Claude Silvente, who lived near Domene, had taken place a few days earlier, on the nights of January 5 and 6. The lad told of a "giant" dressed in a one-piece suit of brilliant color that came out of a mysterious machine. The boy was terrified. Twice the giant had walked toward the boy, who ran away as fast as he could.

Jean-Claude was not the only witness to the machine and its giant occupant when it came the second time, on January 6, and landed in the same spot, covering about five feet of ground. Those with Jean-Claude for the encore performance included his mother, his seventeen-year-old sister, Elaine, and a friend of Elaine's, Marcel Solvini, twenty years old.

The machine, a sphere that looked like "a big red headlight," came down from the sky as though it were going to land on the four of them. The witnesses fled the scene and reported the object and the occupant to the authorities.

CYLINDRICAL HUMANOIDS ON A MINNESOTA HIGHWAY

James Townsend, a nineteen-year-old radio announcer for station KEYL of Long Prairie, Minnesota, was driving west along Highway 27 about four miles east of Long Prairie on October 23, 1965. The time was approximately 7:15 P.M. As the young man rounded a curve at a good speed, he was confronted by a tall object standing in the middle of the road.

Townsend slammed on the brakes, and his 1956-model car skidded to a halt, twenty feet before what he described as a rocket ship. Immediately, the motor, lights, and radio of his car stopped functioning, although the scene in front of him remained illuminated.

The rocket ship was shaped like a cylinder with a blunt taper on one end, and although it was only about ten feet in diameter, Townsend estimated that it was over thirty feet in height. Realizing the consequences of such a find, the announcer's immediate thought was to knock the thing over and retain the ultimate evidence of his sighting. But the engine would not turn over when he turned the key in the ignition.

The tall, narrow craft looked unstable, sitting on protruding fins in the middle of the highway. Townsend thought that he might be able to tip the craft by hand. Jumping out of the car, he advanced on the apparently deserted rocket.

But the young announcer was astonished when three incredible objects moved out to meet him: small cylinders moving on spindly legs no thicker than pencils. Although they had no distinguishing features, Townsend described their movements to be more like those of creatures than of robots.

Townsend had no idea how long he and the objects confronted each other, but he said it "seemed like forever." Then he retreated to his car, and the little canlike beings moved toward their craft. They disappeared in the brilliant beam of light that glared under the main section of the rocket. While the radio announcer watched through the windshield of his car, the light became even more intense, as a humming sound crescendoed in volume until it hurt Townsend's eardrums. Then the rocket lifted off, reminding the radio announcer of a glowing flashlight, and the scene east of Long Prairie, Minnesota, was lit "as bright as day." Once the thing was airborne, the light in the bottom went out.

As Townsend watched the vehicle ascend into the sky, the lights and the radio of his car came on. The car, which he had been unable to start only minutes before, *began running by itself*. Townsend later said he was sure he had not touched the starter, even though the car had been left in "Park" and the ignition remained on.

Unnerved, Townsend turned his car around and sped back to Long Prairie. Without hesitation he went directly to the sheriff's office to report what he had seen. With considerable effort, Sheriff James Bain and police officer Luvern Lubitz were able to calm the excited young man. Both of these men later confirmed that Townsend had obviously been badly frightened. Sheriff Bain described him as "excited, nervous, and shaky," while Lubitz observed that he was "not his natural color."

The first thing Townsend said to these men was: "I am not crazy nor am I drunk; neither am I ignorant."

Bain and Lubitz agreed with the statement, although at first they did not know why Townsend had said it. All who know James Townsend later testified that he is a levelheaded, hard-working young man, not known to drink. Furthermore, he has strong religious convictions, and had spent the summer as a counselor at a Bible camp.

Both men at the sheriff's office listened to his story and acted immediately. Although Townsend was reluctant to return, Bain and Lubitz convinced him that he should take them to the spot where he had seen the strange craft.

After driving out to the spot, all three of the men simultaneously observed a peculiar orange light moving in the northern sky. Lubitz thought it was "more yellow-white than orange, flickering off and on and leaving a sort of yellow tail."

A close inspection of the spot where the rocket ship had been standing showed that three strips of an oil-like substance had been left on the pavement. They were three feet long and four inches wide, running parallel to the highway. Lubitz said that he had never seen anything like those marks left on any kind of surface. After puzzling over it for some time, the men returned to Long Prairie. Sheriff Bain was unable to determine any reason for the marks that had been left on the pavement other than the fantastic tale that Townsend had told him.

SHINY ROBOTS AND TINGLING RAYS

Eugenio Douglas, a truck driver, told correspondents of the Monte Maix, Argentina, *El Diario* and the *O Journal* of Rio de Janeiro, Brazil, that, on the evening of October 18, 1963, on the highway approaching Monte Maix, his entire truck had been enveloped by a brilliant white light. Douglas had only a few moments to speculate about the source of the light before his entire body began to tingle like "the peculiar sensation one gets when his foot goes to sleep."

Douglas lost control of his truck and drove it into a ditch. The beam seemed to "shut itself off," and the truck driver, upon clearing his head, saw that the brilliant light had come from a glowing disc, about twenty-five feet in diameter, which blocked the highway. As he blinked disbelieving eyes, he was approached by "three indescribable beings," which he could compare only to "shiny metal robots."

The terrified truck driver vaulted from the cab of his vehicle, fired four revolver shots at the approaching monsters, and began to run wildly across the open fields. When he at last stopped to catch his breath and look over his shoulder, he saw that the "indescribable beings" had boarded the disc. He was soon to learn that the "robots" had not taken kindly to being fired on.

After the disc had become airborne, the luminous flying object made several passes over the head of the desperately running truck driver. "Each time the disc swooped down on me," Douglas told newsmen, "I felt a wave of terrible, suffocating heat and that prickling sensation."

Eugenio Douglas ran the entire distance to Monte Maix. When he arrived at police headquarters, he was in a near-hysterical condition. As painful evidence to support his incredible tale, his body bore several welt-like burns, which the medical examiner had to admit were "strange and unlike any that I have ever seen." *Acción* reporters from Agrega, Argentina, published an interview with the doctor, in which the physician conceded that he could "offer no explanation for the burns."

OCCUPANT ON CAMERA

Jeff Greenhaw, police chief of Falkville, Alabama, responded to a call about a spacecraft with blinking lights. Greenhaw reported that while he did not find a spaceship, he did see a metallic creature in the middle of the road!

"I got out of my patrol car and said, 'Howdy, stranger,' but he didn't say a word. I reached back, got my camera, and started taking pictures of him," Greenhaw said. He added that the creature ran when he turned on the blue light atop his cruiser.

"I jumped into my car and took off after him, but I couldn't even catch him with my patrol car. He was running faster than any human I ever saw."

Greenhaw described the creature as robotlike, making no sound, and having no features on its face, but a point on top of its head.

Greenhaw was plagued by a series of personal misfortunes after his celebrated encounter—including the destruction of his home by fire. He commented that it was becoming obvious that "someone" wanted him to leave Falkville, but he refused to do so. He reiterated his belief that the picture he took was that of a being from another planet.

A PEWTER HITCHHIKER IN GEORGIA

Mrs. Robinson was driving from Huntsville, Alabama, to Tifton, Georgia, on the afternoon of October 19, 1973. She stopped at a service station for gas and the customary service check, then drove on at high speed.

As she came within twenty minutes of Tifton on I-75, her engine systems all mysteriously ceased functioning. It was about three thirty in the afternoon, she recalls, when she glided off the interstate highway without power steering or brakes.

As the car came to a stop on the shoulder of the highway Mrs. Robinson began to experience what she described as a "strange" feeling. She sensed something weird, and when she turned toward the window next to her, she beheld *it:* a four-foot-tall metallic "man" with a suit that resembled pewter. There was a "bubble" on his head that contained no features except two rectangular slits for eyes.

Although she could not bring herself to look directly at the creature, Mrs. Robinson stated that if the window had been down she could have touched the being.

The bizarre entity walked in front of the car and around to the back, then disappeared. Mrs. Robinson estimated that the elapsed time was about five to six minutes. She felt that the creature was more robot than human, because of its mechanical motions.

Investigators noted that she had not been drinking and was not taking tranquilizers or drugs of any type.

When she was certain that the creature was gone, Mrs. Robinson got out of her car, fearful that it might blow up. She raised the hood to attract passing motorists, and smoke came billowing out.

When a wrecker towed her car to a garage, about one and a half hours later, it was noted that the heat under the hood had been so intense that the engine had almost melted. The metal was so hot "it looked like you could poke your thumb through it." It was another hour and a half before the engine had cooled enough for the mechanic to work on it.

ALIEN WITH A CAMERA

March 1965 was a busy month for aliens in Florida. On March 2, the wire services carried a story datelined Weeki Wachee Springs that told of a Floridian who had had his picture taken by an "outer-spaceman."

John Reeves was a sixty-six-year-old retired New

York City longshoreman, who lived alone in a small house at the site of his trailer court. Reeves liked to go for long walks in the open air and "just think about things."

It was on one of these walks that he saw the UFO across the "flats." He approached the machine slowly, using bushes for cover, being careful not to make a lot of noise.

He was within 150 feet of the disc-shaped thing when a "five-foot-tall being" stepped out from behind some bushes, just 100 feet away from him.

Reeves froze, watching the creature move toward the machine. It was humanoid, Reeves remembered later for reporters, but "strange." Its entire body was clothed in silver-gray canvaslike material, and it appeared to be wearing some kind of mitten. The being wore a bowl-shaped helmet over a human face with extremely wide-set eyes and a very pointed chin.

Reeves got an even better look at the alien's physiognomy when the creature seemed to sense his presence and altered its course to get a better look at the Earthling. It continued directly toward the frightened Reeves until it was about fifteen feet away. Then it reached into "its left side and brought out a black object six or seven inches in diameter."

When the alien raised the object to chin level and began to sight through it, Reeves took off, running. He had seen enough science-fiction movies to know that helmeted creatures from outer space almost always carried deadly ray guns, and he had no intention of being roasted in the Florida flatlands.

Before Reeves had gone far, the object flashed brilliantly, and it suddenly occurred to him that he had just had his picture taken by a tourist from another world.

The alien had advanced no farther but simply stood

still, observing the erratic flight of the frightened man. When Reeves paused, the object flashed in his direction once again.

The last time that Reeves stopped to catch his breath, the alien had turned back toward the spaceship. Then, according to the former longshoreman, the spaceman started up the stairs, which led into the underside of the saucer. When he had entered the machine, the cylinder containing the stairs withdrew into the bottom of the vehicle. A roaring sound became audible; it was shortly replaced by a high-pitched whistle. Within seconds, the UFO had blasted out of sight.

After he was reasonably certain that the flying saucer was not about to make a sudden reappearance, Reeves went back to the area to see if he might not find some evidence to make his story credible to others. He was pleased to note that the being had left a goodly number of footprints in the area and that the landing gear had made deep impressions in the soil.

While he was examining the figure-eight-shaped footprints, Reeves came upon a tightly rolled sheaf of tissue-thin paper. Carefully unrolling it Reeves was amazed to find two sheets of the filmy paper covered with strange, indecipherable marks.

The next day Reeves went into Brooksville, told his story to members of the WFFB radio staff, delivered the manuscript to personnel from MacDill Air Force Base, and returned with reporters and investigators to the spot where he had seen the alien and the saucer. News photographers snapped pictures of the strange footprints and the indentations made by the landing gear.

Reeves submitted to a lie-detector test, and the operator concluded that Reeves was not guilty of deception or lying in giving the answers to the questions asked him in regard to seeing the UFO and the alien. E. J.

Edwards, the polygraph examiners, added: "A further and most significant point of interest is, at the conclusion of the tests, Mr. Reeves first remarked, 'Now, would you like to see the place where I saw the saucer?' The usual reaction of a guilty subject with respect to not answering truthfully is more likely to have been 'Well, how did I make out?' There was, in Mr. Reeves, a complete unconcern about the polygraph test outcome. It is my opinion, therefore, that he was truth-telling in all respects."

Two months later the Air Force returned the alleged alien script with the charge that the whole thing was an obvious hoax. According to Air Force investigators, who had decoded the ciphers, the message read: "Planet Mars—Are you coming home soon—We missing you very much—Why did you stay away too long."

Reeves, confused and troubled by the Air Force's charges, insisted that the sheets which the investigators returned to him were not the same ones which he gave them on March 3.

And there the matter rests: stalemate. Was the sixty-six-year-old retired longshoreman capable of perpetrating an elaborate hoax—complete with strange footprints, landing-gear indentations, a detailed description of an alien, and a convincing manuscript on peculiar tissue paper?

Or was the "hoax" perpetrated on John Reeves as a deliberate move in an alien version of the "reality game"?

CHAPTER SEVEN

The Wretched Uglies

When we are in a state of shock, we are unable mentally to assess what we are observing with any normal degree of accuracy. Witnesses to accidents and crimes argue with one another over which details of the event actually transpired.

Investigators often are able to express only incredulity over the wide variety of descriptions from untrained observers of a dramatic crime. Witnesses to an armed robbery have varied in their descriptions to such an astonishing degree as to report—for the same suspect—differences of six inches in height and twenty years in age. Startled observers have transformed a culprit's gun into a knife, a rope, even a club.

Such extreme reactions to unusual occurrences which shocked or frightened the observers should always be considered when we read the dramatic accounts relayed by the witnesses of paraphysical activity who claim to have seen grotesque monsters issue from grounded UFOs.

Fear of ridicule keeps many UFO witnesses from telling their stories. Seventy-year-old William Bosak of Frederick, Wisconsin, a dairy farmer, is one such example, for he kept what he saw to himself for several weeks before finally telling a local newspaper reporter about it. It was then made public in the St. Paul, Minnesota, *Pioneer Press*.

Bosak was coming home from a co-op meeting at about ten-thirty one evening in December 1974. It was a rather mild evening for that time of the year in Wisconsin, and there were patches of fog on the road, caused by the warm air moving in over the cold ground. He drove slowly, and he kept his headlights on low beam.

About a half mile from home he noticed something on the left-hand side of the road and slowed almost to a stop. A few feet away, he could see what it was very plainly: a strange being in some kind of vehicle.

He told reporters that "The strange being in the vehicle had his hands up as though to show he was surrendering or to show he meant no harm. His eyes showed intense fright!"

It was a very unusual-looking being, according to Bosak, who described it as having hair on the sides of its head that stuck straight out, but no facial hair. He could not tell about clothing, but he said it looked as though it had hair covering its body, which he could only see from the waist up. The fur was a reddish-brown. It's ears looked like a calf's ears and stuck out at least three inches.

The creature was slender and appeared to be about six feet tall, although it seemed taller, since the vehicle was about two feet off the ground. It had a flat face, and the bushy hair and long ears gave it a frightful appearance, according to Bosak.

The arms were covered with hair or fur, like the rest of the body.

"When I got right alongside of the vehicle, which

was about six or eight feet away, he was watching me," Bosak continued. "As I passed it seems the object came right toward my car, and it became very dark in the car."

The object took off when Bosak passed it; it made a swishing sound, and seemed to touch his car. "It did definitely seem as though it came right at me, and there seemed to be a tremendous surge of power."

When asked if the creature resembled a man or an animal, Bosak replied that it mostly resembled a man. He could not tell the color of its eyes, but indicated that they were human-type eyes. Its neck was moderate in length, but he was not sure of the facial features, other than the eyes, and the head seemed normal, human-sized. In general, the description did not fit the prototypical Bigfoot or yeti type of creature.

The object itself was about six feet across. Due to the fog, which obscured its lower section, Bosak was unable to determine whether the object rested on the ground or hovered. Generally, it looked like a chemistry-lab bell jar. It did not appear to have lights of its own, being illuminated only by the headlights of Bosak's car.

Other cases of similar "bell jars" and their "almost human" occupants have been reported. One such case involved an incident about a year earlier, in October 1973, in Cincinnati, where Mrs. Reafa Heitfield reported seeing a strange creature inside a curved glassy enclosure that gave her an unearthly fright.

Canadian UFO Report (No. 21, 1975) told of a September 1973 sighting that was photographed by Mr. and Mrs. Orval Wyman of Columbia Falls, Montana. It showed the same bell-jar enclosure with a similar creature within.

Is this bell jar the method used to drop or "beam down" occupants from a UFO, or is it a method of traveling from another space-time continuum to our own?

Is the bell jar but one more enigma within the vast enigma concerning UFOs? Perhaps we shall know soon—perhaps even sooner than some might think.

MONSTER IN A BUBBLE

A forty-eight-year-old divorcée and her three sons were fast asleep in their mobile home early in the morning of October 21, 1973.

Mrs. R.H. awoke about 2:30 A.M. and got out of bed to get a drink of water. She noticed a light coming through the drawn curtains, and when she pulled them apart she was startled to see a row of individual lights forming an arc not more than two yards from her window.

"Each light was as large as a hand with the fingers spread out," she reported to Len Stringfield, UFO researcher and columnist for *Skylook* magazine.[1]

The lights, six in number, were about four feet above the ground and alternated in color, from vivid blue to silver "as beautiful as Christmas lights." They appeared to Mrs. R.H. to be internally illuminated, casting no radiance to the ground or on a nearby shed.

While the "Christmas lights" hovered outside her window, her attention was drawn to a stronger light farther away, in the parking lot adjacent to her mobile home, in the western part of Cincinnati. A car was parked on the pavement, about ten feet from the home, and partially obscured the bottom of the light source.

Near the light source Mrs. R.H. suddenly saw an apelike creature. She was terrified as she watched for the next two or three minutes. The creature was near the rear of the car, and she thought perhaps it was doing something to the vehicle.

She ran to her son Carl's bedroom and tried unsuccessfully to wake him.

When she returned to the window the creature had moved to a point about thirty-five feet from the mobile home; it was now inside the light source, or bubble of light, which she described as looking like one of the women's umbrellas that come down to the shoulders. The bright light itself seemed to be contained within that shield.

The creature was fully visible, and she described it as having a big waist and no neck. But she could see no distinguishable features about its head other than that the profile showed more a "snout" than a nose. The body was all gray, and equally featureless. Its arms swung slowly, with an up-and-down motion, although there did not seem to be a normal bend at the elbows, and no other part of the body moved.

Mrs. R.H. estimated the bubble to be about seven feet in diameter—large enough to hold several more creatures like the one she described. Although she could see no controls or levers inside the large glasslike bubble, she commented that the creature's arm movement suggested the operation of controls.

While Mrs. R.H. was trying to call the police, the strange bubble and its humanoid disappeared.

Is the creature seen in this bubble or large bell jar in some way related to the origin of so many similar creatures that are called by various names, from Bigfoot to yeti? Perhaps time and more such sightings will tell.

THE ODOR OF MONSTERS

An unpleasant, often nauseating, odor is nearly always a part of what we generally refer to as a "monster" sighting. Such a case involved two young couples who were supposed to be attending a dance, but who were actually parked on lovers' lane on a moonlit night in January 1967, at Elfers, Florida, near New Port Richey.

Shortly after their arrival, one of the girls commented that she smelled a disagreeable odor. Her companions teased her, saying it was just the natural smell of the forest, but she insisted that she was quite familiar with nature, and that this odor was something quite different.

The other three soon agreed that they, too, could smell something that was out of the ordinary, for the odor had become more powerful and had reached a point of being nauseating. Before they could investigate the origin further, an animal about the size of a small ape leaped onto the hood of their car, and the foursome panicked.

"The thing looked like a chimp," one of them volunteered, "but it was greenish in color with glowing green eyes!" [2]

The driver of the car started the motor, and the ape-like thing jumped off the hood and ran back into the woods. The four teenagers decided at this point that it might be best to attend the dance where they were supposed to be, and they told their story to the police officer on duty at the dance.

When he checked, the officer found a green substance on the hood of the car. It was sticky, and it scraped off easily with a pocket knife.

When investigators checked the stories, all four youths related the same chain of events without embellishing on the overall report.

Such sightings are not unusual in the New Port Richey area along the Anclote River. In fact, they have been numerous enough to have led to the creature's being named Florida's "Abominable Sandman." Hunters, hikers, and campers have all reported seeing similar monsters in that area. Some describe it as being six to seven feet tall, heavy, greenish, covered with long hair, and emitting a noxious odor. Perhaps what the teenagers saw was a younger member of a monster family living in the woodlands of Florida.

Earlier, on November 30, 1966, a woman was changing a tire on her car on a lonely stretch of highway near Brooksville, Florida. It was late in the evening—between nine and ten o'clock—when Ms. B. suddenly noticed a strange, unpleasant odor. She next heard a crashing sound in the brush near her, and she turned in time to see an enormous, hairy creature walking toward her.

Fortunately for her, the monster seemed more interested in what she was doing—fixing the flat tire— than in her personally. She told investigators that the creature stood upright, like a man, by the side of the road and just watched her. She was too frightened to scream, and she just stood next to her car and prayed that another motorist would come along soon. Apparently her prayers were answered, for in a short time another car did arrive, but not before the creature disappeared back into the woods.

In later interviews Ms. B. described the monster as having large green eyes, a greenish glow on one side of its hairy body, and an aroma she would not soon forget.

Newspapers in Florida have run numerous accounts of the Sandman, but no one, to my knowledge, has ever actually captured him or mounted his head above a fireplace.

A long-time resident of the Brooksville area, Mrs. Eula Lewis, told investigators that she had been on the trail of the creature since she first saw him in 1964, shortly after John Reeves had spotted a UFO in the same region.

Mrs. Lewis said that she saw the Sandman one evening after hearing a rustling sound in the shrubs near her home as she stood in her back yard. She turned in the direction of the sound and saw an outline of something with a round head and bulky shoulders.

"I moved toward the back door, and it moved toward me!" she said. "I heard loud, thudding footsteps. It had an extremely fast lope and took big steps." It was too dark to distinguish features, but she had the impression that it was quite hairy.

She managed to get inside the house, and neither she nor her husband, Ralph, went back outside that evening. The next morning, when they felt brave enough to venture out, they found several footprints in the area where the monster had been standing. According to Mr. Lewis, the prints were humanoid, not like those of a bear.

Mrs. Lewis did not report a strange odor in connection with the monster sightings, but she could have been upwind of the Sandman.

YETI ANOTHER MYSTERY

A bizarre incident occurred in Turkey on the night of May 14, 1964.

Ismir Bey and his wife were driving along a road that ran adjacent to a railroad track when they spotted a spinning disc in the sky, described by them as "the size of a house." [3]

Suddenly it seemed to plummet out of the sky, and as the two watched it crashed to the ground in a burst of flames. This is certainly one of the few reports of a UFO crashing, and, to add a bizarre twist, a huge, hairy monster was soon seen by the Beys as it scrambled out of the wreckage and headed for safety—straight toward the Beys!

In an effort to protect his wife from whatever fate might befall her at the hands of the monster, Bey flung himself at the beast, and was rewarded for his valor by being pounded into unconsciousness.

Mrs. Bey reported that the monster then flung her husband in the direction of the railroad tracks and ran off into the nearby woods, but apparently it did not try to harm her.

In a later report on this side of the Atlantic, at The Dalles, Oregon, another monster/UFO sighting took place.

According to reports, Joe Mederios, the maintenance man for a trailer court, was watering flowers in front of his office. It was late May 1971, and as Joe looked across the road to a cleft in the bluff he saw what he later described to a sheriff's deputy as "a ten-foot-tall, gray-colored monster with arms that hung quite low." He further described the creature as looking like an ape, and stated that it definitely was not a bear.

The next day, while Joe and three Portland businessmen were holding a conference, they spotted something in the field below the hundred-foot rock bluff. They told authorities that the monster came down from the rocks and walked through the open field across from the trailer court. The creature stopped by a tree, which was later measured at eight feet, giving the foursome an accurate way of estimating the monster's height at about ten feet.

It is interesting to note that Joe Mederios claimed in the report that he had purposely not mentioned the event of the previous day to the other men, "in fear that I'd be called a nut."

More reports were filed in the same part of town, and two nights later Richard Brown, a music teacher at the junior high school, was returning home to the trailer court with his wife when the headlights of their car caught the outline of a figure standing near an oak tree in the field. It was about nine-thirty. Brown raced to their trailer and returned with his hunting rifle, which was equipped with a four-power scope.

The creature remained in the area, and did not move for about five minutes, giving Brown a good opportunity to study it through the scope. His description seemed to substantiate that of Joe Mederios, but, like so many of the elusive Bigfoot-type monsters, the creature disappeared from the area, and nothing conclusive was ever determined about it.

Monster reports are not new; in fact, they antedate the current (since 1947) UFO sightings, having become almost traditions in various parts of the world. In the Himalayas we hear of yeti or the Abominable Snowman, while our own Northwest has long reported sightings of Bigfoot, or Sasquatch. A few years ago the monster of the sightings in Missouri was dubbed MoMo.

The question finally boils down to a few basic theories. Some say the monsters are the missing link between man and ape, while others insist that they are pets or laboratory animals from UFOs used to test the environment of the Earth preparatory to landings by the actual spacepeople. Still others speculate that the monsters themselves *are* the spacepeople.

UFO AND APEMAN IN PENNSYLVANIA

Mr. and Mrs. Philip Arlotta had just stepped into their car, preparing to return home after visiting relatives in Greensburg, Pennsylvania. It was ten o'clock on the evening of May 18, 1975.[4]

Mrs. Arlotta had started the car's engine when she noticed a strange object just ahead of them in the sky. She mentioned it to her husband, who suggested that she turn off the engine—perhaps they could hear something.

The object was moving from east to west, and they described it as being about as big as a cantaloupe, oval, and bright yellow near the bottom but darker near the top. In the darker section were six square windows, which showed a red light behind them.

The Arlottas heard no sound, but they continued to watch the object for about a minute before calling their relatives to join them. Five people witnessed the strange craft as it appeared to move toward them at what they estimated was an altitude of less than one thousand feet.

The craft suddenly made an abrupt right-angle turn

to the left, and at the same time it changed color from yellow to orange before it began gaining altitude.

The witnesses followed the object in the car. As they continued down a back road, they noticed that the object appeared smaller and orange. As they turned onto Route 130, they lost sight of the UFO, but they estimated that they had watched it for about four minutes.

The next evening at about dusk, a lone motorist was heading to his home in Jeanette, Pennsylvania. When he entered that same area on Route 130, something caught his attention just to his left. He stopped his car and backed up.

At a distance of a few hundred yards he noticed what he thought was a German shepherd running—although the movement was more like that of an ape than a dog. After a few seconds, the creature stood up on its hind legs and ran like a man into the woods.

The creature was described as seven or eight feet tall and covered with thick, black hair. The witness, who had been a Bigfoot skeptic in the past, suddenly found himself an instant convert.

The UFO sighting on the first night and the creature sighting on the second night took place within one quarter mile of each other. This was the first creature sighting in this area in more than a year.

LUMBERING GIANT ON PRESQUE ISLE

On July 31, 1966, a number of Erie, Pennsylvania, residents felt certain that "something" had landed on the beach at Presque Isle Peninsula Park.

It was about 10:00 P.M. when patrolmen Robert Loeb, Jr., and Ralph E. Clark came upon a car stuck in the sand at Beach Area Six. Seated in the mired vehicle were Douglas Tibbets, eighteen; Betty Jean Klem, sixteen; and Anita Haifley, twenty-two. They told the policemen that another of their group, Gerald La Belle, twenty-six, had already gone for help, so the officers need not concern themselves with their plight. The patrolmen said that they would make a swing through the area in another forty minutes and check again just to make certain that the car had been freed.

When the patrolmen came through Area Six again, they found that La Belle had not yet returned to the stranded automobile. In addition, according to Douglas Tibbets, some "weird" things had been going on. Something, he said, had landed near Beach Area Seven, and the occupants of the automobile had heard some unusual sounds emanating from that direction. The two officers walked with Tibbets about three hundred yards along the beach, but they could find nothing that might account for the strange noises that Tibbets and the others had reported hearing. Although it was too dark to accurately identify any kind of tracks in the sandy beach, the men were attempting to examine some of the markings when they heard the horn of Tibbets's automobile begin to sound in a steady blare.

When the three men returned to the car, they found the women in varying stages of hysteria. Miss Klem began to run, screaming, down the beach and had to be pursued and calmed by Clark.

Later the events of that evening of terror were put into a coherent sequence by the witnesses.

Shortly after the patrolmen left, at 10:00 P.M., the occupants of the automobile saw a bright light "as big as a house" drop down near Beach Seven. They agreed that the object was "mushroom-shaped" and that they could distinguish rows of lights on the back of it. As the thing landed on the beach, it turned a brilliant red and their "whole car vibrated and shook" from the force of the object hitting the beach. After the landing, the object made a buzzing sound, "like a telephone receiver makes."

As they sat silently in the automobile, the awe-struck passengers could see "rays of light" begin to shine out of the object and sweep the beach "like they were looking for something."

At this point the patrol car reappeared on the scene, its red light flashing, and the rays from the object suddenly dimmed. It was while Tibbets and the patrolmen were investigating Beach Area Seven that Betty Jean Klem saw the "monster."

It was a tall, upright figure, she told the officers, and it completely terrified her. She pressed her hand on the horn and held it there until the creature lumbered off into the bushes.

Miss Klem's eyes were still red from crying when reporters arrived on the scene. Park police chief Dan Descanio was notified, and after interviewing the young people he declared that he considered the matter "no joke." A check of others in the park that night revealed that a number of people had seen a strange object and weird lights late in the evening.

The next morning, investigators found several markings in the sand at the alleged landing site. A number of triangular shapes and skid marks were found, as was a series of tracks leading from the landing site to about twelve feet from where the car had been stuck. A clawlike marking was also found in the area, and a photograph of the print received wide publication.

THE SMELLIES UNDER THE BRIDGE

Robert Hunnicutt was a short-order cook at a new restaurant in Loveland, Ohio, back in the spring of 1955. A report of his humanoid sighting was recorded in *Skylook,* November, 1974, but, so long after the encounter, Hunnicutt was a bit uncertain whether the incident had occurred in March or April of 1955. However, it is the event itself that is of importance here, not the exact date.

Hunnicutt told the police chief, John K. Fitz, that he was driving along Madeira–Loveland Pike when he noticed three men along the side of the road, with their backs to a clump of bushes. He was tired and heading home from work, at about three thirty in the morning. At first he thought the three men were praying beside the road. Curious, he stopped his car to investigate. It was then that he discovered his error—they were not men at all!

The figures were short and stood in a triangular pattern, facing the opposite side of the road. The figure in the front of the triangle suddenly raised its arms above its head, and it appeared to Hunnicutt to be holding some type of rod in its hands—or perhaps a chain. Hunnicutt then saw blue and white sparks jumping from one of the creature's hands to the other, just above and below the rod or chain.

This event was taking place in a rather remote area, with a heavily wooded section just west of the highway.

The creature lowered the rod in the direction of its

feet. To Hunnicutt it appeared as though the humanoid was fastening the rod to its ankles.

Now, as Hunnicutt stood by his car, the three figures turned slightly to the left, to face him. With no sound and no change of expression, the trio started for Hunnicutt.

The headlights of the car illuminated the three humanoids, so that Hunnicutt was able to get a good look at them. They were all about three and a half feet high, grayish, with uniforms about the same shade as their faces. "Fairly ugly," was the way Hunnicutt described them.[5]

They had large, straight mouths without lips, and indistinct noses. Their eyes seemed basically normal, but they had no eyebrows. The upper portion of their heads was bald, with what appeared to be a roll of fat running across the top.

Their bodies were a bit odd, lopsided. According to Hunnicutt, their chests swelled to an unusual bulge on the right side, and their arms were of uneven length, the right one being longer than the left.

The garments above the waist (if indeed they were garments) were skin-tight and showed no line separating them from the skin portion of the humanoids, which was the same grayish color. However, below the waist they wore loose-fitting garments. The hips and waists of the humanoids appeared heavy to Hunnicutt.

Oddly enough, Hunnicutt did not seem to fear the unusual trio. He had been standing on the left side of his car, and he began to walk forward in the direction of the three as they approached him. Hunnicutt described their walking motion as "graceful."

All at once, as though telepathically, Hunnicutt sensed that he should stop. He watched the trio for a few minutes, then left to get witnesses. As he got into his car, he was suddenly aware of an extremely strong odor, which he described as smelling like a combination of "fresh-cut alfalfa and almonds."

As Hunnicutt drove past the three humanoids, he finally began to have a sense of fear for what might have happened. It was nearly 4:00 A.M. by now, and he drove directly to the home of the Loveland chief of police, Fitz.

The chief recalled how he had been awakened by Hunnicutt, who "looked like he had seen a ghost." According to Fitz, the witness told him that he had seen fire coming out of the creature's hands and had smelled a terrible odor. The chief knew Hunnicutt, but he found his story a bit hard to believe. He got close enough to Hunnicutt to smell his breath, and was satisfied that Hunnicutt had not been drinking nor was under the influence of any drug. Chief Fitz agreed to check the area, and he told Hunnicutt to go home.

Fitz got dressed, put on his gun belt, and loaded his camera in case he did find anything. However, after he had passed the area four or five times without spotting any little men, he returned home.

Fitz commented that at the time he did "feel peculiar," and that he also felt that he might have been the "biggest fool in Loveland."

When asked by an investigator what he would have done if he had found the three humanoids, Fitz replied that he would have gotten out of his car and attempted to talk to them. "Someone has to do it sooner or later," he concluded.

CHAPTER EIGHT

The Men-in-Black: UFOlogy's Bad Guys

Even though alchemists in the Middle Ages were experiencing eerie visitations from mysterious scholars and magi dressed in black, the term "Men-in-Black" (MIB) and the attendant terror syndrome did not come into being until September 1953, when three dark-garbed men were alleged to have silenced Albert K. Bender, the director of an international flying-saucer bureau.

According to UFO lore, Bender had gained access to data that he felt provided integral clues for ascertaining the origin of flying saucers. He jotted down an outline of his suppositions and mailed it to a trusted friend. When the three dark strangers appeared at Bender's door, one of them held that letter in his hand.

Bender was informed that he had stumbled on the correct solution to the UFO enigma, but that he remained ignorant of the full details. Bender became ill after the three men had provided him with the complete UFO story. Such knowledge, he realized, would bring about dramatic changes in all earthly constructs.

Mass hysteria would grip the populace. Albert K. Bender agreed to give up his research.

In 1956, Gray Barker published Bender's story—minus the detailed revelations the MIB had given Bender about the UFO enigma—and told of several other UFOlogists who had been silenced after they had come too near the truth about flying saucers. Barker ended *They Knew Too Much about Flying Saucers* with an ominous presentiment: "I have a feeling that some day there will come a slow knocking at my own door. They will be at your door, too, unless we all get wise and find out who the three men really are."

By 1966, dozens of other flying-saucer researchers claimed to have experienced an eerie, sometimes violent encounter with the MIB, who came to be known as the "strong-arm agents" of the UFO mystery. After the heavy UFO flaps of 1966–67, MIB activity increased in direct proportion to the sightings of unidentified aerial lights.

Investigator-journalist John A. Keel commented that the victim of the MIB often appeared to have been subjected to "some sort of brainwashing technique" that left him in a state of "nausea, mental confusion, or even amnesia" lasting for several days. "The menace is not in our skies," Keel warned. "It is on the ground, and at this moment it is spreading like a disease across the country and the world."

A short-lived television series, *The Invaders,* had had a tremendous impact on flying-saucer researchers. The dramatic stories, which told of one man's efforts to alert a complacent world to the presence of extraterrestrial aliens, was said to be based on thinly veiled truth.

When Frank Edwards died after having written two highly successful books on UFOs, the seeds of paranoia were scattered on powerful winds of fear. In spite of obituary notices which declared that Edwards's death was due to a heart attack, the UFO buffs opted for induced cerebral hemorrhage, the "invaders' " favorite method of disposing of humans who had come too near the actual facts of their alien presence and their hostile mission. Serious UFOlogists found themselves in a maelstrom of ostensible terrorist activity. The UFO silencers seemed to be everywhere.

Percipients of UFO activity were being told by scowling, eccentric "Air Force officers" not to talk to flying-saucer researchers. Photographs of UFOs were being confiscated by dark-complexioned men dressed in black.

UFO buffs blamed government agencies. Government agencies blamed over-eager, amateurish civilian UFO investigative groups. Nearly everyone, at least on some level of troubled consciousness, wondered if it might not really be Them—aliens from outer space.

Pentagon spokesmen were quoted as admitting that they had checked out a number of MIB reports and were prepared to go on record that the terrorists "are not connected with the Air Force in any way." Nor would any other U.S. security group claim the MIB. Spokesmen from each of the major federal agencies stated firmly that none of their agents were empowered to demand surrender of private property by any law-abiding citizen, to threaten him, or to enter his home without court orders or warrants. The spokesmen added that the UFO silencers were committing a federal offense by posing as military or government agents. But the harassment of UFO percipients continued nationwide. Men and women were left nauseated, confused, feverish after their ordeals with threatening inquisitors.

MIB activity had been on the decline until after the flap of October 1973. Then once again the patterns of fear and chaos were repeated. It would appear that, whoever the MIB might be, the ominous tricksters have presently resumed their troublesome antics with renewed vigor.

"Brad, I just cannot believe that this is really happening to me!" The voice on the telephone was vibrating more with bafflement and tension than with fear, but the concern was very evident. The young man and his fiancée had suddenly found themselves engulfed in the living nightmare of the MIB phenomenon.

"No, Sam," I replied. "And three years from now you might not be certain that it really *did* happen to you. But right now . . ."

"Right now, *I know!*" Sam said emphatically.

Briefly stated, the MIB are a phenomenon within a phenomenon. In several instances, those men and women who have witnessed UFO activity—or such related manifestations as monsters, Bigfoot creatures, and phantom entities—have suffered a peculiar kind of personal harassment. Sinister voices have whispered threats over the telephone and warned researchers and witnesses to terminate specific investigations. Those who have taken photographs of UFOs have been called on by rather unusual individuals who confiscated the pictures and the negatives—often by claiming government affiliation.

In the majority of cases, victims of the MIB have described their inquisitors as rather short men, probably five foot six or less, with dark complexions and somewhat Oriental features. When pressed for more complete descriptions and details, the witnesses have stated that the MIB had eyes that were noticeably slanted, but slanted in a way somehow different from Japanese, Chinese, and other Orientals. Some witnesses have mentioned pointed or peculiarly misshapen ears. Many percipients have noted that the MIB have difficulty in speaking properly because of short-windedness. In some instances their speech patterns are suggestive of several afflicted asthmatics gasping for breath in mid-sentence.

Some of the MIB are more silly than threatening. Certain percipients of UFO activity have commented that they felt as though they were being interrogated by daffy Three Stooges-type characters, who were only assuming the roles of tough guys.

In *The Mothman Prophecies,* John A. Keel adds the observation that the MIB are obsessed with time, often beginning an interrogation by asking the percipient what time it is. The MIB also very often appear to be out of place in the period in which they have materialized, and they often utilize hilariously outmoded slang expressions.

After a percipient has experienced a confrontation with the MIB, his home utilities and appliances often become traitors in the employ of the mysterious strangers. Telephones ring at all hours with threatening or nonsensical mechanical voices. Television and radio programs are interrupted by alien signals. Network video and audio are blotted out, to be replaced by images of robed, sometimes cowled, figures, who instruct the saucer sighters to cooperate and to keep all UFO information confidential. In exchange for this silence and cooperation, the mysterious entities promise the percipients key roles in marvelous projects which will benefit all mankind.

From 1966 to 1970, hundreds of UFO investigators, contactees, and chance percipients of UFOs claimed to have been visited by ominous strangers—usually three, usually dressed in black—who made it painfully clear that they would violently enforce their orders to discontinue flying-saucer research or to surrender all photographs or artifacts. Often the threats were punctuated with the assertion that cooperation with the MIB was essential for the good of "your family, your country, and your world."

In the March 1975 issue of the *New Atlantean Journal* (6290 Thirty-fourth Avenue North, St. Petersburg, Florida 33710), Michael Talbot points out that Eastern mysticism has an interesting analog for the MIB phenomenon, known as the Brothers of the Shadow. According to Eastern adepts, Talbot states, the Brothers of the Shadow are:

> . . . cunning and evil; intent upon keeping any student of the occult from finding out the proverbial answer. In mystical jargon this answer is the "Veil of Isis," and is synonymous with the "Great Secret" of Maeterlink. In occultism, as in the UFO problem, there is recorded a constant barrage of psychic hoaxes. The Brothers of the Shadow, like the MIB, are known for threatening students of the occult whenever they get too close to lifting the Veil of Isis. As Madame Blavatsky says when referring to the Brothers of the Shadow, they are "the leading 'stars' on the great spiritual stage of 'materialization.'"

Paranoia may become contagious, but I have been convinced through personal investigation—and first-hand experiences—that the phenomenon euphemistically known as the Men-in-Black is very real and that its victims are not simply suffering from particularly eerie delusions. Although the characters and stage settings differ in each of these bizarre psychodramas, the basic script remains unchanged. The MIB phenomenon is very much like a macabre traveling repertory theater that specializes in multilevel audience participation.

Take the experience of the young intern who, for purposes of this book, I call Sam.

It all began for Sam and Mary (also an assumed name) when Sam was closely involved in the investigation of a number of creature sightings in the Eastern state where they live. On one occasion Mary accompanied the researchers, and during the course of the evening she was somehow put in a trance.

That evening, in a strange dream, grotesque entities told Mary that she was wanted by them. She was told that she must leave Sam—Sam was wrong for her. In fact, he was so wrong that if she did not join them, they would have him beaten and killed. In dreams on subsequent evenings, Mary saw grim, dark-complexioned men beating Sam until he was dead.

One evening she was awakened from such a violent nightmare by the ringing of her telephone. When she mumbled an answer, the voice asked: "Now are you ready to come over to our side?"

The telephone became an instrument of fear. It would ring at all hours, only to provide its startled listener with peculiar beeps and threatening voices which spoke in mechanical monotones.

Once when Mary was alone in her home, a man appeared at the door, flashed credentials, then asked to question her concerning the strange telephone calls which she had been receiving. Mary let him into the house.

"I later determined that his credentials were phony," Sam told me. "Mary may have lost some time here, I'm not certain. She's been going into trance more and more often."

Mary's trances were usually prefaced by a headache, a pain in the back of her neck, then a lapse of consciousness. A trained nurse, Mary was able to recognize the symptoms of the approaching trances, but she seemed powerless to prevent their onset.

The main reason why Sam had called me was to

ask if the MIB ever proved to be physically harmful.

"I believe not," I told him. "Some people have suffered black or red eyes, but that appears to be connected with a peculiar electromagnetic aspect of the phenomenon.

"The important thing is not to play their game, and especially do not cast them in the role of badmen! It is this dualism that comes so readily to mankind that sets up the warfare structure with the phenomenon. If you permit hostility, then that is what you will receive!"

In my opinion, the phenomenon is neither good nor evil. All activity is the manifestation of a single source. How the MIB conduct themselves depends in large part on the percipient with whom they are interacting. They provide immediate feedback, like malign echoes: Cry out in fear and they'll give you good reason to fear them. I am convinced that this aspect of the larger phenomenon is constructed primarily as a teaching mechanism. The important thing for anyone who finds himself a victim of the negative aspects of the phenomenon is to begin at once to structure his reality to exclude the MIB, to break their hold on his reality construct.

Many victims of the MIB, on some level of consciousness, may actually enjoy the threats, the danger, the excitement of the perverse drama in which they have permitted themselves to play a central role. The only physical danger may lie in heeding some of the vile commands and forecasts and permitting oneself to act out the eventuality of a self-fulfilling prophecy.

Several days after the conversation recorded above, I received a letter from Sam, which detailed the phenomenon's concentration of activity on Mary and its perpetual suggestion that she leave him and become "one of them." Sam complained that the greatest interest of the phenomenon seemed to lie in its resolution to break up their relationship. Mary was slipping ever more frequently into the trance state. At times she seemed almost to be possessed.

I sent Sam the following letter, which I reproduce here to present certain perspectives and guidelines for others who may find themselves so afflicted:

It is incredible how the phenomenon travels about like some cosmic repertory theater, changing its character actors, but retaining its basic multilevel plot structure. I say this not to minimize the morass in which you and Mary find yourselves, but, hopefully, to enable you to maintain always your perspective.

Your erstwhile tutors have now moved the action into the personal arena. The penny-dreadful terrors have been abandoned, and the much juicier area of personal relationships is being mined. *Don't play the game!* As John Keel has always emphasized, belief is the enemy. The phenomenon conforms to your belief structure.

Traditionally, the phenomenon has been particularly interested in lovers and the male-female relationship. Fairies had an obsessional interest in bringing some couples together—and in breaking up the romances of other couples. In all cultures, girls approaching puberty or women experiencing menstruation have found themselves the seat of paranormal manifestations.

The phenomenon has introduced a new phase to teach you to remain above quarreling over petty matters and nit-picking personal imperfections. But they have also moved into the personal arena as a part of their compulsive interest in male-female activities. The entities sometimes act like the dirty old men with raincoats on their laps who attend porno movies. Don't provide them with such entertainment. *Don't play their game!*

MIB activity seems to have been increasing since the UFO flap of October 1973. Perhaps this is due to some cyclic pattern of which we have no knowledge. Maybe it is happening because of the societal transformation which seems to be upon us. The essential fact is that we can seize on the potential to learn valuable lessons from the phenomenon, rather than permitting paranoia to run rampant.

Although I did not become as deeply embroiled in the MIB skirmishes of 1966–70 as my fellow researchers did, I did tread on the periphery of the vortex of swirling, nightmarish games. And from time to time, as I extensively detailed in *Mysteries of Time and Space,* I did enter the court where the contest was being played in frightening earnest. I endured the "smellies"—vile, odorous attacks of some invisible entity—and the poltergeistic plunderings of my office.

But then I stumbled on two clues that may just solve the whole puzzle of who the Men-in-Black really are!

One night as I sat in my office, desperately working at the typewriter to meet a publisher's deadline, I heard the sound of heavy footsteps at the top of the stairs. A quick glance told me that no one was there. A favorite portrait of Edgar Allan Poe fell to the floor. I became irritated. Papers began to rustle off to my side. A single sheet became airborne.

I had had enough. I looked up from my typewriter, rolled my eyes upward in disgust, and shouted: "Just cut it the hell out!"

Everything stopped. It was like walking into a crowded, noisy room, and everyone suddenly stops talking. I went back to my writing without taking further notice of anything other than the work at hand.

Every kind of intelligence, regardless of how high or how low, wants to be recognized. Nothing shuts up any thinking entity faster than being *ignored*. But I hadn't ignored it. Rather, I had *commanded* this poltergeistlike force. I had refused to go along with its framework of reality, and my own change of attitude —from passive fear to rage—had apparently done the trick. The cessation of odd activity in my office was so abrupt that it was almost as though some kind of lesson had been terminated. Could it be that some intelligence was trying to teach me something all along?

Is it possible the MIB are tutors, here simply to teach us that it *is* possible to fight City Hall, to command other forces by a sheer effort of will? Of course, they threaten, but when confronted with a firm refusal, or—as in my case—defiance, they simply slink away. It would almost seem that they are deliberately bullying us into revolt, using childish, annoying methods to get us to stand up and take charge of our own lives. Is this, in fact, the point of their lesson, if lesson it is?

As I theorized in *Mysteries of Time and Space,* the MIB are suggestive of the mythological figure common to all cultures and known generically to ethnologists as the Trickster. The Trickster plays pranks on mankind, but often at the same time he is instructing it or transforming aspects of the world for the benefit of his human charges.

Most cultures view the Trickster as a primordial being who came into existence soon after the creation of the world. A number of Amerindian tribes referred to their Trickster figure as "Old Man," because they saw him as someone who was ageless, as old as time.

The Trickster is usually viewed as a supernatural being with the ability to change his shape at will. Although basically wily, he can at times behave in a very stupid, childish manner, and often may end up as the one who is tricked. The Trickster lies, cheats, and steals without compunction. Often he seems to be the very essence of amoral animalism.

Carl Jung saw the Trickster as a mythological shadow figure who provides the reverse image of the saint, the angel. The animalistic Trickster serves as the impish, dark opposite of the bright conscious mind and establishes a balance without which psychic wholeness may not be achieved. This certainly sounds like the poltergeist or MIB. And yet, most cultures do not cast the Trickster in the role of the devil. He is often seen as a once-high god cast down from the heights of pure divinity. He is usually portrayed as the entity who brought fire to mankind (in the Prometheus legend he pays for this vital gift to *Homo sapiens* with his own eternal pain).

In an article on the Trickster figure in *Man, Myth and Magic,* Douglas Hill writes that the many roles of the Trickster blend and fuse: "Trickster is comic relief; he is psychic catharsis on a deep and vital level; he is a hero whose own evolution perhaps mirrors that of mankind toward a higher consciousness and social maturity. And, embodying all these essentials, he is deathless—no ethnological museum piece, but alive and flourishing today as in the primeval past."

The Trickster figure often appears in the guise of a culture hero. To the Amerindians, the Trickster appeared as a wily coyote or clever warrior; to the Norse and the Greeks he assumed the role of a mischievous (but hardly demonic, and often helpful) god; but to our culture, devoid of traditional heroes, the embodiment of wily amorality—one who can lie, cheat, steal, even kill, and still be defending a cause he considers noble—would be none other than an international spy.

Was it only coincidence that James Bond films were emerging at the same time that the Men-in-Black were beginning their terrorist campaign? The MIB were almost always described as dressed completely in black —a pretty obvious symbol—and often with their dark hats pulled low. Regardless of the nationality of the victim, the MIB were nearly always said to be "foreign-looking," with peculiar accents. The MIB, in one sense, become interchangeable in characterization with the agents of SMERSH, James Bond's nemesis.

In other words, once the prototype of the Men-in-Black had been fashioned—as a result of either paranoid imagination or an actual visitation—men and women involved in UFO research could have sustained the *idea* of the MIB.

The yoga concept of the *tulpa* maintains that a thought form can assume life independent of the psyche "feeding" it with emotions and mental emanations. According to certain Eastern metaphysicians, *similar* thoughts, emotions, and mental emanations can add to the strength of the *tulpa,* enabling it to accumulate power and grow. The *tulpa* can manifest apparent solidarity and vigor, and yogis claim that they can even carry on intelligent conversations with these creatures of their own minds. The duration of a *tulpa's* life and its vitality are in direct proportion to the tension and energy expended on its creation.

Even a small bit of ego indulgence could "feed" the thought form of a menacing Man-in-Black and begin to grant strength and independent life to a sinister *tulpa*-like creation. And if, as yogis teach, similar thoughts, emotions, and mental emanations can add to the *tulpa's* power, certainly the rampant paranoia of UFOlogists and flying-saucer buffs might have fashioned independent thought forms of nearly unrestrained growth.

Ever alert to changes in the *Zeitgeist,* the spirit of the times, the MIB phenomenon has added a few new scenes and some additional supporting players since the October 1973 UFO flap. Pause to reexamine the case of Sam and Mary. In addition to the spy motif, which was so popular in 1966–70, the phenomenon has also begun to employ the mechanisms of possession. Why? Quite possibly because of the enormous popularity of the book *The Exorcist* and its subsequent film version.

In the majority of MIB reports which I have received in the past few months, visits by the once-ubiquitous three dark-garbed men have been largely supplanted by trance states, whispered commands that the afflicted become "one of them," shouted expressions of desire for the percipients' actual physical bodies. In addition, stigmatalike rashes and wounds have appeared on the percipients' flesh, often taking the form of letters of the alphabet or esoteric symbols. The percipients' normal facial expressions and basic characters alter in front of friends, so that the percipients appear to be possessed.

There is no question in my mind about the basic scenario having remained the same—the telephones still act up; the basic threats remain standard; the levels of procedure are relatively unaltered—but the phenomenon panders to fads and popular interests, just as a hack playwright does. And why not? It desires to communicate in the most readily recognizable guise available. If it ever thinks about such matters, it is probably bemused at the fact that the popular mechanism of 1975 is very much the same as that of 1475: demons, exorcists, and the drama of the perpetual warfare between the forces of Light and Darkness.

But I repeat: *The only "exorcism" that is needed is the full realization that one has been led into a silly game.* This realization must then jolt the victim into determined action, in which he shouts, in essence: *Cut it the hell out!* Once this cathartic action has been accomplished, he then returns at once to a meaningful life.

I have heard it theorized that when a person feels himself set upon by marauding entities and begins to cross himself and recite prayers, he jams the frequency in his brain on which the entities have been trying to establish contact and control. It may well be that a determined demand to "Knock it off!" might have the same frequency-jamming effect and permit the percipient of the phenomenon to regain control of his own cerebral equipment.

But I do urge that we concentrate on the positive aspect of the Trickster/poltergeist/UFOnaut/MIB so that we might construct a reality game that we will have a fair chance of winning.

And we can start playing it immediately! Fire existed, certainly, before Prometheus brought it to mankind. It was simply the *knowledge* of fire that he offered us. I believe the powers of telekinesis, teleportation, etc., *already* exist within us. It is merely the *awareness* of these powers that the Tricksters are trying to impart. The Tricksters may provide us only with fragments. It may be almost totally up to us to move the pieces around until a pattern begins to form. Then, one day, we will have full realization that the final square in the great cosmic reality game lies before us—awaiting our next roll of the dice.

And while we are lining up for our turn at the cosmic dice table, perhaps we might gain some encouragement from these words by F. W. Robertson: "Evil is but the shadow that in this world always accompanies good. You have a world without shadow, but it will be a world without light—a mere dim, twilight world. If you would deepen the intensity of the light, you must be content to bring into deeper blackness and more distinct and definite outline the shade that accompanies it."

CHAPTER NINE

UFO Encounters May Be Hazardous to Your Health!

I have often speculated about the process of selection involved in the UFO experiences: Why are some men and women selected for what would appear to be authentic visionary experiences, while the great majority of percipients must settle for glimpses of lights in the sky? Why do certain witnesses interpret the interaction with UFO intelligence as enlightening, while others react with horror and loathing?

There are other instances in which it is difficult to determine whether the percipient has somehow failed some kind of cosmic test that could have qualified him or her as a revelator—or has been singled out for some perverse experiment.

Don Worley of Connersville, Indiana, conducted a lengthy investigation into the case of a woman who had been an unwilling channel for UFO-associated paranormal manifestations for many years. A full reading of the lengthy transcripts provided me by Worley seems to indicate that a certain mental confusion afflicted the woman, in addition to the psychic chaos that swirled around her. I feel, though, that one should not too readily consign the woman's experiences to the realm of psychological aberration. As the reader will see, every time the woman appears to be "getting it together" a manifestation of some sort appears to flash a brilliant light in her eyes and the psychic maelstrom begins again.

Here, greatly edited, are excerpts from Worley's investigation of what he calls the "eerie Ann Adams case."

Worley: How long have you lived in this house?
Mrs. Adams: Three years.
In other words, you have endured this manifestation in other homes where you have lived, not just here?
Mrs. Adams: Yes, in every one that we have lived in for the past fifteen years.
How many homes is that?
Mrs. Adams: I think this is about the seventh. We rented all the time until we bought this. We're trying to tough it out if we can.
Since the phenomena have followed you about, the history of this house probably isn't particularly pertinent, but do you know anything about the people who have lived here?
Mrs. Adams: There was a couple named K——who lived in this house. The man died in that back room. The lady was sick for a while and died here.
Did this house have any strange noises before you moved in?
Mrs. Adams: No, the neighbor lady who took care of the old couple that died said that there was never anything like that here.

But after we moved in—well, it got so bad last summer that I went to a woman who was a medium. There were nights that we couldn't sleep. It seemed like the doors banged all night. The windows went up and down. There was the sound of walking in the hallway upstairs.

Your husband heard these sounds too?

Mrs. Adams: Oh, yes. And I'd wake up and the room would be filled with a real strong perfume that would just about suffocate me.

For a few years nothing bothered me; then we moved out in the country on V—— Road. Terrible groans started up almost at once. Any time of the day or night this groaning would cut loose in the house. We all heard it. Even the kids saw things. They saw people in the yard at night, and when they went to see who it was, the people would vanish.

One night I heard a baby crying. I set out after the cry, and I kept hearing it, and I kept following it clear across fields and creeks until I came to a little patch of woods. Then it stopped. [The sound of what seems to be a baby crying is often heard prior to UFO, poltergeist, and other paranormal manifestations—AUTHOR.]

Right after that my brother and his wife had a baby boy, who lived for only a few months. I always thought that maybe my hearing the baby's crying might have been associated in some way with my little nephew's death.

Did you see anything else that sticks in your mind as important?

Mrs. Adams: I saw what is called a troll. It was in the road down below the house. I was fixing supper one afternoon, and I looked out and there it was. It had on overalls, some kind of shirt, and long gray hair down its back. It was about this tall [she indicated about three feet]. I started to run out of the house to chase it, but it ran over a hill and disappeared.

The next thing happened just before my daughter-in-law was killed, in a car wreck. I had been nervous for weeks. It's usually in the summertime, June, July, and August, that these things happen to me the most. This one hot night, I was lying downstairs on the couch when all of a sudden I jumped up and ran to the door, as if I was waiting for something to happen.

I had stood there for only a short time when I had a vision of a police car driving up to our house with its flashing red light shining in my eyes. The light hurt my eyes, and I heard a man's voice shouting something about death.

I got so upset that I went to Dr. K——. I told him about the phantom police car and the red light. He could see the red marks around my eyes, but of course he wouldn't believe my story. He sent me to the hospital for five shock treatments. [UFO percipients are often victims of conjunctivitis and other types of eye inflammation—AUTHOR.]

You mean the red marks around your eyes that I can still see first appeared after the visitation of that phantom patrol car?

Mrs. Adams: Yes, that was in 1965. Right away my eyes started itching and bothering me, and then these red ridges appeared. They've been there ever since. [That is, for *five* years—AUTHOR.]

But anyway, the hospital didn't help me, because I continued seeing the red lights flashing, even while I was under treatment.

Then I found out that my daughter-in-law was driving my son to work in the mornings, and I knew that she was going to be the member of the family who was going to be killed. I told Dr. K—— this, and he wanted to put me back in the hospital.

But on the thirty-first of August that year, she

was killed instantly as she was returning home after taking my son to work.

How did your family react to the memory of your premonition after it had been fulfilled?

Mrs. Adams: They didn't want to talk about it.

What about this walking sound that you hear?

Mrs. Adams: It sounds like it starts back at the front end of the hall and comes to the top of the stairs. I think the footsteps sound like a male.

Are there any cold drafts or cold spots that you have noticed?

Mrs. Adams: Oh, yes. And once I saw what appeared to be a man in a heavy sweat shirt walking up the stairs. I thought at first it was my husband, but then I heard him coughing in the downstairs bathroom.

Have you ever seen any lights?

Mrs. Adams: Yes, I have awakened sometimes and I've seen lights. That happened last night.

[Worley accompanied Mrs. Adams down to the basement workshop, where he and his research assistant were able to speak to Mr. Adams. Worley comments: "One gained the reliable impression that the man of the house could tell us a great deal more, but he preferred to keep busy at his work in the basement and ignore things he couldn't understand." Worley gained admissions from Mr. Adams that he had heard screams on two occasions, walking sounds quite often, and the noises of the stairs squeaking and various doors slamming.]

Mrs. Adams: Every Christmas we've been in this house there has been something strange happen. It seemed like there was some kind of presence here last Christmas. After everybody left and went home that night, my husband and I sat alone in the living room. It was real cold that night, and of course the doors were closed up tight.

All at once something that howled like the wind came in through the front door. My husband looked around at the front door, but I knew it wasn't open. It howled through the house and went out the back. It was just like some wind blew through the house. For some reason I started crying, and I cried for three days. It was just like some kind of presence had come in.

Worley telephoned Mrs. Adams again on June 4, 1970. He was told by the subject that there had been no developments since December 1969, with the exception of an animal-like scratching that had been heard several times near an upstairs door. Mrs. Adams told Worley that she was staying "close to God" by Bible reading and by an association with a fundamentalist religious group that was sending members to call on her.

On September 8, 1970, Worley telephoned again. He learned that there had been relative peace in the Adams house, with the exception of several nights in July. Mrs. Adams had prayed, and the disturbances had ceased.

Worley's last report was carried out on June 13, 1971: "All is peaceful at subject's home. However, I thought I detected a note of tiredness or sadness. Subject prays and reads Bible. She will call me if she gets into difficulty. I hope and pray her tormentor of so many years is gone for good."

We are all familiar with the inability of the human ear to hear sounds emitted by a dog whistle, and we have been recently made aware of many types of rays that cannot be perceived by the human eye. It would appear that we possess an extremely limited awareness of the totality of existence in what we like to think of as our reality.

As we probe deeper and wider with increasingly sophisticated and elaborate instruments, we may well begin to wonder if we will ever be able to delineate the parameters of our actual reality. We may one day soon, with remarkably sensitive cameras, be able to photograph the phenomenon of unseen hands that nevertheless leave prints, of invisible feet that issue clearly the sound of their tread on creaking floorboards, of mysterious forces that have haunted man since his earliest glimmerings of intelligence. Indeed, our technology might one day soon answer the paraphysical question of what lies "beyond."

At our present stage of knowledge, it appears that there may be perils for those who are inadequately prepared for Third Kind encounters or unscheduled excursions into the unknown.

Gladys Worthington was awakened at about 2:00 A.M. on June 21, 1975, by the unmistakable pressure of a hand on her throat.

Her husband was at work on the night shift at the plant, but her four dogs were sleeping downstairs. Why hadn't they warned her? Understandably startled, Mrs. Worthington probed the darkness, desperately trying to see her assailant.

"I could see nothing," she said later. "But I felt a tingling sensation running up my body from my toes. I tried to scream, but I couldn't. As quickly as it came, the sensation went."

Mrs. Worthington lay back down. Perhaps she had been troubled by a nightmare so terrible that her conscious mind had already snuffed it from memory. After all, weird things had been happening in their house on Salvin Street, Croxdale, Durham, England. Both she and her husband had got the "shivers" witnessing objects moving about of their own accord. And then there was the time when they had caught sight of a ghostly white figure.

Uneasy, but more relaxed, Mrs. Worthington closed her eyes. Perhaps she could get back to sleep. Things would look better in the morning.

Then, once again, with terrible pressure and terrifying purpose, the hand was at her throat!

Mrs. Worthington struggled upright to face her attacker, but, as before, there was no visible molester. She lay awake for the rest of the night, not wanting another replay of the frightening scene.

When morning came, Mrs. Worthington told London reporters: "I got up thinking I had been dreaming. I went to the mirror to make up my face, and got a terrible shock. There were five bruises like pressure marks from a thumb and four fingers."

Mrs. Worthington's doctor agreed that the marks on her throat had been made by heavy pressure ("apparently a hand"), but he would not accept her story about being strangled by a ghost.

When twenty-six-year-old Barry Lacy did not return for lunch on a summer's day in 1969, his wife went looking for him in the field that he was plowing. Two hundred yards from the tractor, which was still upright, with the motor running, Lacy lay sprawled with serious head injuries. His flask of coffee lay crushed beneath him.

Lacy was rushed to Battle Hospital, Reading, Berkshire, England, where it was determined that he had suffered a fractured skull and paralysis of his left side. At last report, the young farmer was completely paralyzed and had suffered total loss of memory in regard to the circumstances of his accident. His case has been investigated by police, attorneys, farm-machinery experts, insurance-claim investigators, Lacy's fellow farmhands, and his employer. No one has been able to come up with a single clue as to what happened to the young farmer who set out one fine summer day to plow a field.

On July 7, 1973, a man about forty years old was found unconscious near Port Angeles, Washington. Among other injuries, he had suffered a broken shoulder and knee. He had been battered so severely that he did not know his own name, recognize his own face, or have the faintest idea where he lived. No identification was found on the man.

On September 27, 1974, police investigators in Southall, Middlesex, England, were confronted with a baffling variation on the classic locked-room mystery. Aubrey Packham, sixty, was found battered to death in a bus company's office. There was absolutely no sign of a break-in, no evidence of a fight. Nothing had been stolen from either the firm or Packham. No motive and no murderer have been found. There remains only the unsolved mystery of a man found beaten to death in a neat, well-ordered office.

An invisible hand that leaves finger marks on a woman's throat; a young farmhand left paralyzed, with a fractured skull; a stranger so badly beaten that he has lost all knowledge of his identity; a man found battered to death in an office that bears no testimony of an intruder.

In each of the above mysterious attacks, the assailant seemed somehow invisible to human sight yet capable of dealing terrible violence to the body. There are cases, of course, in which wounds appear mysteriously through the psychosomatic mechanism known as stigmata. However, in these instances the victim, on at least an unconscious level, often has sought the physical markings as evidence of his extreme piety or demonstrable proof of the intensity of his mystical experience.

It is true that Mrs. Santuzza Campbell was alone on a cliff at Bridlington, Yorks, when something laid her low with a fierce blow to the head, but there is no evidence that she was meditating or seeking a mystical experience. No clue could be found that could account for who or what had clobbered Mrs. Campbell. It was theorized that something might have fallen from an airplane, but if this were correct, her head would have been mashed, rather than lumped.

In such unexplained mystery attacks, those investigators bold enough to consider paranormal or Fortean explanations have adduced the vast body of poltergeist literature: accounts of men and women being pummeled, poked, punched, and prodded by invisible intelligences. Others have theorized that such occasional violent acts might be the work of entities who have interacted with mankind for centuries, sometimes manifesting themselves as woodland elves, other times as occupants of UFOs. Although generally curious rather than cruel, and mischievous rather than malicious, both of the above-named entities have sometimes been reported as a bit feisty and occasionally downright pugnacious.

Hostility may not be the motive in such mystery attacks. Or perhaps we should say that the majority of these alien interactions with us do not seem negatively shaded by overt acts of hostility. But just as we have certain small boys in our species who throw rocks at frogs and drown pet cats to test for "nine lives," other-dimensional entities may have immature or seemingly motiveless manglers among their number. A less-optimistic viewpoint has it that just as we have serious researchers who kill thousands of laboratory animals in the name of science, some interloping intelligence might be willing to sacrifice certain of our species in an attempt to learn more about us physically and psychologically.

Since we seem, by and large, to be a particularly nasty and aggressive species, there may be some risk involved in any kind of interaction with us. Those who would launch experiments utilizing members of our species may find themselves victims of our primitive but effective weapons.

In the February 1970 issue of *Fate* magazine, J. Russel Virden writes of an incident that occurred when he was nine years old. In the middle of a cold November night in 1943, Virden and his brothers were awakened by his mother's hysterical screams. Their father was on duty at a post near Hattiesburg, Mississippi, so the three boys attempted to calm her, but she kept sobbing: "His face was green, green, I tell you!"

Before the puzzled and frightened children could determine *whose* face was green, they heard the booming roar of their neighbor's 12-gauge shotgun. The man had been alerted by the woman's screams and had fired at what he thought was a prowler. He insisted that he had hit the intruder square in the back, but that the man had just kept running.

"Someone came with a flashlight," Virden writes, "and we followed the path the intruder had taken to the highway . . . There on the asphalt were large splatters of *yellow* blood!"

In reconstructing the incident for her neighbors, Mrs. Virden told of having been awakened by a loud pounding at the front door. As she arose to answer the door, knocking began at the back door. When she started toward the back door, the pounding resumed at the front door.

Angry and exasperated, she ran to the front door and pushed aside the curtain: "Through the window she saw not a human being but a manlike creature with a bright green face. The leering, other-worldly face had shocked her into hysterical screaming."

Virden concludes his account by stating that the alien man was never seen again, but that everyone in the small community who had seen the yellow blood or who had heard his mother's testimony "believed they had been visited by a being from some other world."

It should be emphasized that Mrs. Virden saw her alien in 1943, four years before the modern era of UFOs began with Kenneth Arnold's sighting near Mount Rainier. It would be most interesting to learn how many other humanoids were running about fixing the archetype of the "little green man" in the collective unconscious before the Great Mystery "officially" began in June 1947.

But even though "They" might occasionally "get theirs" when they are beating on some of us and scaring the bejabbers out of others, all too often it is one of our species who perishes as a result of their playing a bit too rough.

Early in March 1974, eleven-year-old Ian Salt set out from his home in Solihull, to watch the airplanes at Birmingham Airport. Later, he was found drowned in a hidden pond well away from his expected route.

The boy had crossed a plowed field on his ill-fated journey, and forensic experts were able to determine that he was being chased. A careful study of his tracks indicated that something had caused the youngster to panic and run wildly across the field; crashing through a hedge, he fell into the pool.

But no other set of tracks was ever reported, and the case was soon dropped from inquiry. What had so frightened the boy on his way to go airplane watching? Had he confronted his own green man?

About a month later, Garnett Oliver was found drowned in four feet of water in a well at Field Farm, Partney, Lincolnshire. The eighty-five-year-old farmer had engaged in a lively chat with a friend just an hour before his body was discovered.

The heavy concrete slab that covered the well had been removed, but the coroner could find no marks on the body that would indicate a fall into the narrow well. Nor was there any suggestion of coronary failure, or any evidence that a second party had pushed Oliver into the well. The death was filed under "unexplained."

Perhaps some of those British water sprites and undines are not very friendly. Just a few days before Ian Salt was mysteriously drowned in the hidden pond, the bodies of two women washed ashore a few yards apart at Lossiemouth, Morayshire. The man who discovered the bodies remarked that it appeared as if "the tide had gone out and left them exposed on the sand." Police were unable to identify the bodies or discover if they were in any way connected.

A week after Ian Salt was drowned, three farm-workers found the body of a man floating in the Bristol Channel at Lilstock, near Bridgewater, Somerset. Police were unable to identify the body in spite of a nationwide inquiry.

Nor were authorities able to identify the bodies of a woman found in the Manchester Canal and a man found in the Methly River near Leeds approximately two weeks after something frightened Ian Salt. The man had been cleanshaven and well dressed, and had an eyeglass case bearing the name of a local optician, but all clues drew blanks.

Students of UFOlogy and strange phenomena are familiar with the series of mystery attacks that stalked the village of Warminster in England. The invisible menace began plaguing the townspeople on Christmas Day of 1964 and continued to molest them for several years. At the same time, sightings of UFOs and strange lights in the sky became common in the area.

Typical of the reports issuing out of Warminster during the reign of terror is that of Eric Payne, who was then nineteen years old. Payne was returning home after a date with his girl friend. Mist rose off the marshland to greet him. Then . . .

Just short of the apex of the bend, I heard a loud buzzing. It was not from telegraph wires. I'm not dead sure from which direction it came—it was overhead so quickly that it took me by surprise. As it hovered over me, it sent shivers up my spine.

Imagine a giant tin can, filled with huge nuts and bolts being whirled and rattled above your head . . . Then . . . I felt a rain of sharp stinging blows on my head and cheeks. A wind tore at my hair and hurt my eyes, it was so fierce. My head and shoulders were pressed down hard. I tried to fight off the invisible attacker. Just before it lashed down at me, I saw no aircraft in the sky, no plane lights or anything.

For some time I staggered about in the road, then managed to sink to my knees on a grass verge at the roadside. The ground was wet, but that didn't worry me. All I badly wanted was to rid myself of that choking, clutching "Thing."

Mrs. Madge Bye was aware of a crackling sound

above her head as she walked to church on Christmas morning, 1965. She felt herself hurled against a churchyard wall and "pinned there as though by invisible fingers of sound." Mrs. Bye was then frozen into a temporary state of shock.

The weird crackling sound paralyzed a small dog and set a nine-year-old girl's limbs to jerking about when she attempted to carry her pet indoors.

David C. Holton, a botanist, geologist, and biologist, told of seeing a flock of pigeons suddenly killed in flight for no apparent reason. He examined the birds as soon as they hit the ground and found that almost instantly rigor mortis had set in.

The accounts at Warminster go on and on. If the incidents were not hysterical in nature and spread by psychological contagion, then a number of elements seem consistent with other reported instances of UFO "hostility." There are also certain aspects of the encounters that would seem consistent with electromagnetic phenomena. Combining the seemingly paranormal with the electromagnetic and microwave manifestations so often reported in association with the phenomena, it would seem that close approaches of UFOs, either accidental or intentional, might be very hazardous to our health.

It is no secret that various governmental agencies, both civilian and military, have been experimenting with various rays that would be capable of doubling a man's life span or of paralyzing or slaying entire populations—depending on the use to which the rays would be put. It has been theorized that if one could use microwaves to excite the organic molecules of the acid adenosine triphosphate (ATP), which is essential to the body's muscular system, one might be able to direct another's muscles from a distance! Scientists involved in such research have stated that by utilizing masers (microwave amplifying devices) they could extend the effectiveness of a paralysis ray to almost any distance on Earth and in space. A weapon making use of ATP's critical microwave resonance frequency would produce effects ranging from temporary paralysis to sudden death.

Once such a molecular manipulator was developed to a high level of sophistication, the ray could immediately charge an individual's muscular system with power and enable him to accomplish incredible feats of strength. Negatively, the ray could flood the muscles with too much energy and cause them to "lock" against one another. In this case, the man would become literally musclebound, completely paralyzed. In still other applications of the ray, certain muscle groups, such as the cardiovascular system, could be singled out and paralyzed in order to bring about near instantaneous death.

I am not suggesting that UFO intelligences possess such paralysis and death rays and are deliberately directing them against us. The discharge of such microwaves might be a byproduct of a UFO's entering our dimensions of reality. Just as jet aircraft have left shattered windows below them as a byproduct of their breaking the sound barrier, so might a dramatic response from the muscular system of a percipient of UFO activity be the side effect of extraterrestrial or multidimensional craft entering our space-time continuum.

Gregory Wells of Wilson, Ohio, claimed that on March 19, 1968, a beam of light emanating from a UFO knocked him down as he was getting a bucket of water. According to Wells, the UFO appeared suddenly and hovered above a large tree, about thirty feet off the ground. The beam shot out of the object, knocking him to the ground and setting fire to his jacket and a circle of surrounding grass. Wells's mother rushed to aid her son as the UFO moved away. The young man suffered minor arm burns.

On October 1, 1968, near Lins, Brazil, a bulldozer operator stated, he saw an automobile-sized UFO near his machine as he went to work at 6:00 A.M. The man reported seeing three beings with human faces peering out at him from behind windows in the object. According to his testimony, a yellow ray shot from the craft and dazed him. Although he was woozy, the bulldozer operator claimed that he saw two UFOnauts leave the object and scoop up handfuls of dirt. When they had their specimens and reentered the vehicle, the UFO made a rapid ascent.

On August 19, 1965, in East Liverpool, Ohio, four neighborhood boys were camping out in a back yard when a large UFO swooped down and began to hover above them. The boys ran in terror to their homes, but one of the lads, who was a bit more stalwart, stayed outside to watch the spacecraft for just a few seconds longer. As he stood there, a door at the bottom of the craft opened and emitted a "light ray" which struck the boy on the side of the head. The boy's hearing was impaired for a long period before it returned to normal.

On September 7, six-year-old Barry Bruns of Durand, Wisconsin, came home complaining about the "thing" outside that had hurt his ears. When Mrs. Edward A. Bruns went to investigate, she saw a strange object about thirty feet long hovering about four feet off the ground between her home and an orchard two hundred feet away. Because of her close association with her husband's construction business, Mrs. Bruns felt that her estimate of the object's length was accurate.

On Saturday night, September 17, Joe McFarland

and Edward Alcorn, both about seventeen years old, went out into the woods in Rockcastle County, Kentucky, to get a piece of wood for a school woodworking project. Almost immediately after sitting down to rest for a minute, the two teenagers began to complain of feeling "weak and woozy."

Later, Joe McFarland told the Mount Vernon, Kentucky, *Signal*: "We both noticed it was getting light around us . . . then it got real bright and we both looked up. About twenty-five feet above us was a bright circle of light . . . It looked like the overhead lights in an operating room of a hospital. The light was about thirty feet across. It was only on a few seconds, then seemed to die out, and it was dark again. We didn't hear any kind of sound."

The two boys ran down the hill, stumbling and receiving scratches from briars. Alcorn's brother and sister and a friend thought the boys were joking until they accompanied them to the crest of the hill, where they could all see a mysterious light in the sky.

"We could also see another, smaller light. We could see the brighter light between the trees . . . it would blink once, then three times. Then it would go dark. Then it would blink once, then three times, and go dark."

"I can tell these boys told a straight story," said a state police officer who listened to McFarland and Alcorn give their report. "I think they told exactly what they saw. But what they saw is a mystery. It is interesting that others in different areas of Rockcastle County have seen strange objects and lights, and those others are unrelated to these people and this incident."

Professor Felipe Machado Carrion tells of a grisly incident that involved a healthy, robust farmer in the state of São Paulo, Brazil, who was struck by a beam of light from the sky. Although the incident took place in 1946, it was published for the first time in the December 1971 issue of the French *Phénomènes Satiaux* and was later reprinted in the March–April 1973 issue of the British *Flying Saucer Review*.

According to Carrion, forty-year-old João Prestes Filho was stunned and knocked to the ground by the mysterious beam of light. He made his way to the home of his sister, where numerous friends and neighbors came to aid him.

Eyewitnesses later told authorities that Prestes showed no trace whatever of any burns, either major or secondary. But within a matter of hours the once-vigorous farmer began *literally* to deteriorate before the eyes of his startled friends.

Although at no time did he appear to feel any pain, ". . . Prestes' insides began to show, and the flesh started to look as though it had been cooked for many hours in boiling water. The flesh began to come away from the bones, falling in lumps from his jaws, his chest, his arms, his hands, his fingers . . . Some scraps of flesh remained hanging to the tendons . . . Soon every part of Prestes had reached a state of deterioration beyond imagination. His teeth and his bones now stood revealed, utterly bare of flesh . . . Now his nose and ears fell off, sliding down his body on to the floor. . . ."

Six hours after Prestes had been struck by the beam of light, he was dead. The rapidly disintegrating man had not even been able to reach the hospital before he was nothing more than an eye-bulging skeleton, with strange, guttural sounds issuing from between his clenched teeth. He died still attempting to communicate details of his experience.

Police investigation yielded no worthwhile clues. No marks were found at the site where Prestes was struck by the light. But, Carrion concludes, "There were further sightings of the lights in the air, lights performing capricious, unexpected, inoffensive evolutions in the night skies. . . ."

A close approach by a UFOnaut may also produce physiological effects on the human percipient, though none as ghastly, it would seem, as the case of João Prestes Filho.

On September 1, 1965, a Peruvian laborer, who is said by one reliable informant to be a "very responsible person and incapable of inventing such a thing," told of being suddenly overcome by a "strange sensation" which led him to a certain area of the airfield at which he had been working. It was about 5:00 A.M. when an oval disc descended from the sky and settled on the field a short distance from the man.

Held in place by the unusual "sensation," the laborer saw an alien emerge from the spacecraft. Although only about three feet in height, the being was humanoid in all respects, except that, as in so many other occupant cases, the alien was reported to have a head about twice as large as would be proportionate for its size.

The humanoid paced before the laborer and seemed to be trying to communicate with him by waving its arms and emitting short, rapid barking sounds. At last it apparently gave up, and reentered the UFO.

On July 1, 1965, while working his field near Valensole, France, Maurice Masse was startled to see an object that looked like an immense rugby ball standing among his plants.

As Masse approached the object, which he described as about the size of a Renault Dauphin car, he saw two little "men" investigating one of his plants. Aside from their shortness (they were about the size of an eight-year-old child), their large heads (three times the size of a normal adult's head), and their lipless mouths, Masse observed that they were human in appearance.

The farmer continued to approach the little men, intent on conversing with them. When they suddenly noticed him, however, one of the aliens pointed a tube at Masse and rendered him completely immobile. Freed of further distractions, the two little creatures continued to chatter together, in a language unfamiliar to the farmer, as they examined the plant. Although they occasionally sent a mocking glance toward Masse, the Frenchman at no time felt that the little men wished him any real harm.

It was not until a quarter of an hour after the spacecraft left that Masse was able to move once again. Prominent citizens substantiated the farmer's tale by telling newsmen that they had seen the strange tracks that the little men had left and the holes that had been made by the space vehicle's six extensions. Masse has a solid reputation in the mountain village, and a gendarme told reporters that the police were not inclined to regard the incident as a joke.

On August 13, 1967, at 4:00 P.M., Inacio de Souza and his wife, Maria, were returning home to their farm at Santa Maria, between Crixas and Pilar de Goiás, state of Goiás, Brazil, where he was the manager. When they arrived, they saw a strange object shaped like a basin, only upside down. It was thirty-five meters in diameter.

Between the craft and the house there were three strangers. It appeared to Inacio that they were nude, but his wife suggested that they were wearing close-meshed clothing that was pale yellow. They seemed to have no hair.

When the "men" saw Inacio and his wife, they pointed to both with their forefingers and started to run in their direction. Inacio shouted to Maria to run to the house, and he shot the nearest intruder just as a beam of green light hit him on the chest. Inacio fell to the ground and Maria returned to defend her husband, grabbing his rifle. At this, the humanoids fled to the craft, which took off vertically with the noise of a swarm of bees.

For the next two days, Inacio was nauseous (as if from radiation poisoning). He felt numbness in his entire body. His hands trembled, he burned, and he was finally taken to Goiánia. The doctor there attributed the "burning" of Inacio's body to accidental poisoning, probably from eating a noxious plant. Then Inacio related his remarkable encounter to the doctor. Surprised, the physician ordered various tests, including a hemogram. Upon seeing the results, the doctor concluded that Inacio had leukemia or some other blood alteration, and estimated that Inacio had no more than two months to live.

Inacio lost weight and became frightfully thin. At the end, he was only skin and bones. He had pale-yellow blots all over his body, and he felt strong pains. He told his wife to burn his bed, mattress, and clothes if he died—which occurred less than sixty days after the incident.

On June 14, 1968, Pedro Letzel, a motel owner in Chile, returned home to find his nineteen-year-old daughter, Maria, sprawled unconscious on the floor. Upon being revived, Maria told a remarkable story of being attracted by an area of brilliant illumination in the hallway of the house. As she watched in bewilderment, an apparently male being about six feet tall materialized before her.

As the blond entity raised his right hand, Maria became dizzy. Her vertigo ceased when he lowered his hand, which was partially covered by a large ring.

The being seemed friendly, and he mumbled incessantly in an unintelligible murmur. He also made noises suggestive of laughter, but at no time did he appear to move his lips. The entity remained visible for several minutes, apparently enjoying the one-sided conversation. When he finally vanished before her eyes, Maria fainted.

At almost the same time that Maria Letzel was an unwilling hostess to her mumbling guest, Catalicio Fernandez was entertaining alien beings clad in brilliant green suits in his home in Buenos Aires. His entities, too, seemed friendly, but he too complained that he would feel dizzy whenever one of them would raise an arm toward him.

"I could see nothing in his hand," Fernandez said. "There was no ring, signaling ball, or crystal, such as other people who have seen these beings have reported."

Mary Geddis, aged twenty-one, of Albany, Ohio, claimed to have seen a tall ghostlike "thing" as she returned home from an evening class at Ohio University on October 16, 1973. A few moments later she saw a "bright white light" bobbing over a field, only twenty-five to thirty feet above the ground when it was closest to her.

While she was preparing supper, neighbors arrived home and stated that they had sighted something strange in the sky. Mary's friend Joe went outside to discuss the matter with them, and that was when Mary saw a little "electric man" looking at her around the corner of the open door.

"It was like the electric man they have on the Co-op signs," she told George M. Eberhart. Mary Geddis felt no attempt at communication; she said that the entity "just stared" at her for perhaps ten seconds.

She said that it did have a face, but that it had

"spiky things at the top and sides of the head." The entity was less than three feet tall, with "stumpy" arms. Ms. Geddis reported seeing no legs, and she later described the being as an "energy form."

What might have happened if Mary Geddis had seized the peculiar peeping Tom? She might have ended up with a burned hand, just as Petter Aliranta, a twenty-one-year-old Finnish forestry worker, did.

According to a report by Tapani Kuningas in the September–October issue of *Flying Saucer Review,* two forestry workers confronted a "little green man" dressed in a one-piece suit with a lenslike opening in its "astronaut" helmet. As the entity was floating toward an opening in a UFO, Aliranta grabbed the heel of its right boot with his bare right hand. "However, he had to let go of the foot right away as it burned like a hot iron [the wounds caused by the burning on the thumb, forefinger and inside of the hand were still clearly visible two months later]. At the same time, Aliranta automatically took a couple of steps backward, so the entity was able to glide back into the craft undisturbed."

The encounter had lasted only three minutes, but Aliranta and his friend, Esko Juhani Sneck, were unable to walk away from the UFO landing site for nearly an hour. They were amazed and awed by the experience, but they also actually felt stiff and had some difficulty in moving. By the next day Aliranta's hand was so bad that he could hardly hold his ax. In spite of his pain, he and Sneck went about their work as usual—except that they spent a good deal of time looking over their shoulders. Two months later, Aliranta told journalist Kuningas that he was afraid to walk alone in the dark, even though no further incidents had occurred.

I am certain that nearly all of us can identify with the young forestry worker's response to a most unsettling experience. But Petter Aliranta can count himself fortunate that he received only a burned hand from an entity that may have been capable of leaving him battered or paralyzed in the woods, to be classified as another victim of a mystery attack.

On the other hand, "victim" and "attack" are emotion-charged terms, whose meaning may depend almost solely on perspective and point of view. Certain individuals' unfortunate sense of timing may have brought them to the wrong place at the wrong time. And it may be only man's limited perspective that suggests that certain acts may be hostile or evil.

Surely, if one is severely burned by accidentally touching a high-voltage wire, he may consider electricity evil. This would not be the opinion, however, of the millions of men and women who utilize electricity to heat their homes, toast their bread, illuminate their homes, and power countless tools and appliances. To those who have not been badly shocked or horribly burned, electricity is good.

In actuality, electricity is neither evil nor good. It is an impersonal energy that we are somehow able to harness and define, even though no one knows for certain what it really is. As Sir Philip Sidney once remarked, "there is nothing truly evil, but that which is within us; the rest is either natural or accidental."

CHAPTER TEN

Interrupted Journeys
and Cosmic Kidnappers

Whenever our explorers and scientists visit a new land, they are certain to return with flora and fauna from that region. From Caesar with Cleopatra to our astronauts and our planetary probes with moon rocks and Martian soil, mankind has steadily amassed trophies from faraway places with strange-sounding names. Perhaps the desire to "show and tell" is universal.

The case of Betty and Barney Hill has been covered in the press, numerous books, and a recent television movie. It would seem that even the person with only a cursory interest in UFO matters would be familiar with this case. As a brief memory-jogger, however, I will outline the details of this prototypical "interrupted journey," which has culminated in a mystery concerning a star map that has proven to be mind-boggling.

Betty and Barney Hill, a couple in their forties, were returning from a short Canadian vacation to their home in New Hampshire when they noticed a bright object in the night sky of September 19, 1961.

Barney stopped the car and used a pair of binoculars to get a better look at it. The light soon showed the well-defined shape of a disclike object that moved in an irregular pattern across the moonlit sky. Barney walked into a nearby field to get a better look. He saw the object plainly, and he was able to see what appeared to be windows—and from the windows, people looking back at him!

Barney was terrified as he got back into the car and raced down the road. Then, for some reason, he drove the car down a side road, where they found five humanoids standing in their path. Suddenly unable to control their movements, Betty and Barney Hill were taken to the UFO by the humanoids.

The details of the Hill's story were elicted only under hypnosis, for they had a complete loss of memory concerning the nearly two hours following the initial contact with the humanoids. The Hills were returned, unharmed, to their car, at which time the humanoids told them they would forget the abduction. The UFO then rose into the air and disappeared from sight, and the Hills continued their journey home, oblivious to the whole event.

The remarkable encounter would probably have never been brought to light except for two factors: the inexplicable dreams they both had following the events aboard the UFO and the unaccountable two-hour gap in the journey home from Canada.

Barney, a mail carrier, and Betty, a social worker, continued to be puzzled. Finally Betty sought the help of a psychiatrist friend, who suggested that the memory would return eventually—in a few months. But the details of that "interruption" remained lost until they were revealed through the aid of hypnosis, conducted by Dr. Benjamin Simon, a Boston psychiatrist, in weekly sessions.

Under hypnosis the two revealed what allegedly happened that night. The individual stories of Betty and Barney agreed in most respects, although neither knew what the other had disclosed until later.

Both told of being well treated by aliens from space, much as humane scientists might treat laboratory animals. They were then given a hypnotic suggestion that they would forget what had happened aboard the UFO. Their induced amnesia had apparently been broken only when they were rehypnotized.

The two hours aboard the craft consisted of various physical examinations, but the key to the whole event, and the factor that may be conclusive in giving the story credibility, is the star map that Betty claims she was shown while aboard the UFO.

Under hypnosis in 1964, Betty drew her impression of the map. Her map concurred with other, professionally drawn, star maps, which is in itself remarkable, since Betty had little understanding of astronomy. But there was a big bonus factor—her map showed the location of two stars called Zeta 1 and Zeta 2 Reticuli, allegedly the home base of the space travelers. The existence of the two stars was not confirmed by astronomers until 1969—eight years after Betty "saw" the star map aboard a "spaceship." As an added zinger, the two fifth-magnitude stars are invisible to observers north of Mexico City's latitude.

The case of Betty and Barney Hill remains one of the most baffling and thoroughly documented of Third Kind encounters.

INTERRUPTED JOURNEY IN FRANCE

Ms. Helene Giulana, a twenty-year-old French civil servant, was driving her car en route from Valence (where she'd seen a movie) to her home in Hostun on National Route 531 on the night of June 10, 1976, when, at 1:30 A.M., the headlights went out and the engine stopped. She was wide awake; the gas tank was not empty; but her automobile had inexplicably stopped running after she crossed the bridge of Le Martinet.

Then she saw a strange, luminous orange mass standing on the road about fifty feet in front of her car. Ms. Giulana locked all of her doors and, frightened, covered her eyes with her hands.

When she had recovered her courage enough to glance again at the road, the thing had disappeared. With some hesitation, she tried the ignition. The car started at the first turn of the key. Relieved, fighting back panic, Ms. Giulana started for home. Because of her distraught condition, she took the longer way home, by way of La Beaume d'Hostun. But, even so, she should have been within the security of her own rooms within thirty minutes.

Ms. Giulana was astonished to note that it was 4:00 A.M. when she reached her home. How had the thirty minutes become more than two hours? How long had she sat before the luminous orange mass in her immobilized automobile? What had occurred during those two hours of which she has no memory?

Ms. Giulana said that she was at first very reluctant to recount the details of her experience, for fear of being ridiculed. But she knew that she was respected quite highly in the town of Hostun, where she is employed at the Town Hall. Depending upon her credentials and her reputation to support her through the crisis of transient mockery, Ms. Giulana was determined to share her account of what may have been her very own "interrupted journey."

ABDUCTED BY MONSTERS AT PASCAGOULA

October is often a very slow month for UFO activity, but 1973 proved to be an exception to all rules, starting with the report of two Mississippi fishermen who told authorities that they had been taken aboard a flying saucer that looked like a giant fish.

Charles Hickson, forty-five, and his fishing companion, nineteen-year-old Calvin Parker, were fishing from an old pier in the Pascagoula River, near the city of the same name in Mississippi. The men reported seeing a fish-shaped object, emitting a bluish haze, approaching from the sky. The craft landed, and the men allegedly were taken aboard by three weird creatures with wrinkled skin, crab-claw hands, and pointed ears. The men claimed to have been examined, then released.

Sheriff Fred Diamond of Pascagoula told investigators that the two men were scared to death when they reported to him, and that he feared they might be on the verge of heart attacks.

Their story was interesting enough to draw the attention of Dr. J. Allen Hynek of Northwestern University in Chicago, who had served as scientific consultant to the Air Force's Project Blue Book, and Dr. James Harder of the University of California, who had the men hypnotized. They then revealed their traumatic experiences aboard the strange craft.

Harder commented, "These are not imbalanced people; they're not crackpots. There was definitely something here that was not terrestrial, not of the Earth."

"Where they are coming from and why they are here is a matter of conjecture, but the fact that they were here on this planet is beyond reasonable doubt," commented Hynek, who added: "The very terrifying experience of the two men indicates that a strange craft from another planet did land in Mississippi."

Hynek concluded that although the men could be hypnotized, their experience was so traumatic that it was necessary to progress slowly with them.

This is the story the two men told:

They were fishing for hardhead and croakers from an old pier near the Schaupeter Shipyard, a sun-bleached skeleton of a barge drydock, at about eight o'clock the evening of October 11. Suddenly a UFO hovered just above them. "There was me, with just a spinning reel, and Calvin went hysterical on me. You can't imagine how it was," said Charles Hickson.

According to the report of the sheriff's office at Pascagoula, Hickson related that the luminous, oblong craft landed near them. Three creatures paralyzed him, floated him to their craft, placed him in front of an instrument that resembled a big eye, then put him back on the pier.

Calvin Parker was not able to add much to the report. He apparently fainted when the creatures approached the two men, and he said he did not know what happened inside the strange craft. After a couple of days, the two men refused further interviews with the press.

Following this report, literally thousands of UFO sightings began cropping up from all over the United States, followed by more sightings from every corner of the globe. The October flap was underway!

More reports of UFO sightings came from other residents of Pascagoula that night of October 11, then from Gulfport, Mississippi. Over to Tallahassee, Florida, where two residents reported unidentified lights crossing the night sky of Leon County. North to Dayton, Ohio, where six more objects were spotted skimming over the Buckeye State. And on October 5, a week before the two fishermen had their experience in Pascagoula,, a park ranger near Tupelo, Mississippi, reported seeing a saucer-shaped UFO with red, green, and yellow blinking lights.

COSMIC KIDNAPPERS

On September 16, 1962, Telemaco Xavier allegedly was taken away by an alien party. Xavier was last seen walking home along a dark jungle trail after attending a soccer match in Vila Conceicão in northern Brazil. A workman at a nearby rubber plantation told authorities that he had seen a round glowing object land in a clearing. Three men got out of the fiery vehicle and grabbed a man who was walking along the trail.

Rio de Janeiro newspapers quoted authorities who had discovered "signs of a struggle where the worker said the fight had taken place." To the Brazilian newspapers it seemed evident that "Mr. Telemaco Xavier was kidnapped by a flying disc."

Was the Brazilian added to a collection of Earth life which was to be scrutinized, evaluated, and analyzed in some alien laboratory?

On August 13, 1965, two Renton, Washington, sisters came to work at 7:00 A.M. to get an early start in Yas Narita's bean field near Kent. Ellen and Laura Ryerson had barely entered the bean field when they noticed that three "workers" were already walking in the area. The teenaged sisters had not been in the field long when they discovered that the three strangers were more interested in *them* than in gathering beans. Even more frightening was the girls' discovery that their three fellow bean-pickers were not human beings.

The three strangers had white, domed heads and protruding eyes. They were between five feet two inches and five feet five inches tall. The flesh of their expressionless faces had very large pores, and their complexions were "gray, like stone." The three aliens wore sleeveless purple V-neck jerseys with white shirts underneath.

Fortunately for the girls, the three strange "men" were easily outdistanced and appeared to be without weapons. Ellen and Laura were able to get back to their automobile, and they sped away to make their report to the Washington State Patrol.

In the Andean town of Santa Barbara, no less a personage than the lieutenant governor claimed to have seen two men about three feet tall walking through the snow near Lake Ceulacocha. The aliens seemed to disappear in a brilliant flash after they had walked about for a few minutes. Hundreds of peasants in Huancavelica, Peru, were terrified later that same day when five UFOs buzzed their village for about three minutes.

From the village of Torren, Santo Time, Argentina, comes the story of UFO occupants who returned on successive evenings in February 1965 in an attempt to kidnap residents of the small farming community.

The first attack came on a very dark night, when a UFO landed in full view of a small group of terrified farmers. Two strange beings about six feet in height emerged from the craft and walked directly to a farmhouse, where they tried to drag off the farmer who lived there. Rallying to their friend's defense, the other farmers managed to thwart the aliens' kidnap scheme and drove them off.

On the next night, when the saucers landed to carry out their kidnap mission, the farmers opened fire on them with their guns. Although the aliens' space suits seemed to protect them from the farmers' bullets, they seemed weak physically and were quite easily discouraged from further attempts at seeking quarry from the village.

No one on either side of the bizarre interplanetary brawl seemed to have been seriously injured; however, the farmer who had entered into prolonged physical contact with the celestial kidnappers did come down with a strange skin disease.

FOUR ENCOUNTERS FOR THE SPANISH TRUCK DRIVER

"Maxi Iglesias does not seem very imaginative. If he is lying, he does it to perfection."

Thus stated reporter Angel Gomez Escorial, writing in *White and Black,* a Spanish magazine, concerning a young truck driver who reportedly witnessed UFOs on four separate occasions and had two Third Kind close encounters!

On the night of March 20, 1974, twenty-one-year-old Maximiliano Iglesias Sanchez was driving his truck past the village of Horcajo on his way back to Lagunilla when he noticed a very strong white light some two thousand feet ahead on the highway. At first he assumed it was another truck, or perhaps a car. He switched his headlights to high beam several times, to signal the other driver to dim his own lights. The bright light remained almost blinding in its intensity. Its brilliance forced Maxi to pull his truck to the side of the road.

The bright light eventually dimmed to about the power of a fifty-watt bulb. Maximiliano then continued to drive toward the light. When he was about six hundred feet away, Maximiliano discovered that the thing was indeed something *very* strange: Without warning, all the lights on his truck went out and the motor stopped. The area was illuminated only by the now dim light of the craft.

Sanchez described the object as having a metallic structure of either platinum or steel. It seemed quite solid, and it had smooth edges without rivets or openings of any kind. It was thirty to thirty-six feet in diameter and rested about five feet off the ground on three round landing pads.

"It was a light like I have never seen before" was how Sanchez described the dim light, which seemed to be uniform on all surfaces of the UFO.

He then noticed a second, similar "ship," as he called it, above and about fifty feet to the right of the first.

As if from nowhere, two beings appeared in front of the grounded UFO. They moved together, and began motioning to each other "like the tourists do." They looked at Sanchez, and one pointed at him. At that, one of the humanoids turned around and disappeared to the right of the first UFO, while the other remained to watch the young trucker.

Soon the other being returned. The two entities looked at each other; then both disappeared to the right of the ship. Soon, it slowly raised in the air with a slight humming sound.

Sanchez described the humanoids as about six feet tall and wearing close-fitting coveralls. The material of their coveralls was brilliant, like the ship, and appeared to be made of a rubbery material. The occupants' walk was "normal," not like that of a robot, and their arms and legs seemed to be proportioned like a human's. As hard as Sanchez tried, however, he could not describe their facial features. The encounter had occurred at night, and he was never closer than six hundred feet to the entities.

When the first UFO reached the altitude of the second UFO, the two objects remained motionless in the air. Sanchez then decided to leave. His truck started right away, and the lights worked once again.

But he had driven only a short distance from the twin UFOs when curiosity got the better of him. Sanchez stopped his truck and climbed down from the cab to study them. He noticed that the illuminated ship had dropped down to the site where it had been before.

At this point, and for the first time, Sanchez registered fear. He took off as fast as his truck would carry him, and he drove straight to his home in Lagunilla, where he went to bed immediately without eating.

The following day Sanchez told the story to his his neighbors, but he found that they did not believe him. However, the son of his employer told Sanchez he believed that the event had happened, for it was similar to the experience a commercial traveler claimed to have undergone near Seville.

That afternoon, March 21, Sanchez drove to Pineda to deliver a load of construction material. While there, he made his customary visit to his sweetheart, Anuncia Merino.

Sanchez told her and her family what had happened the night before. They insisted that he stay with them for the night. It was getting later, and they were afraid for him to make the trip through that area again.

He did not take their advice, however, but headed back home to Lagunilla.

At about 11:15 P.M. he arrived at the site of

the previous night's UFO/humanoid sighting. Once again he saw a bright light ahead of him. Sanchez was convinced that the entities would do him no harm, as on the night before. Again he drove to within about six hundred feet of the light. That night, however, the light was produced by not one but three UFOs.

As before, the truck lights went out and the engine quit—this time with a backfire! One of the UFOs was resting on the highway; the other two were just off the road to the right side of Sanchez, one behind the other. All three were illuminated with the same soft light he had noticed the night before—or, rather, earlier that same morning.

Suddenly four humanoids appeared and walked to the center of the craft resting on the highway. The four looked at Sanchez as though studying him, communicating with one another through gestures. The beings pointed at Sanchez, then started walking in his direction.

Sanchez, fearing the motives of the four, began running along the highway. The four entities increased their pace. Sanchez started cross country, with the four gradually gaining on him. When he came to a ditch, he jumped into it.

The move to evade his pursuers seemed to work: They had lost him—for the time being, at least. He could watch them from his muddy vantage point as they circled in search of him. Although they were often as near as fifty feet, he could still not make out facial features—a matter that seemed to bother him when he reported the incident.

Finally the four strangers left, and Sanchez felt it was safe to vacate his hiding place.

He started walking, and he was soon within sight of the lights of Horcajo, which he estimated at about a mile away or less. He sat down and smoked a cigarette to calm his nerves. He rested for perhaps ten minutes, then returned to the area where he had left his truck, feeling that by now the spot would be deserted. He was wrong, for the three ships were still there—although he did not see the four humanoids.

As Sanchez reached the truck, something bothered him. The door was closed; he remembered that he had left it open when he departed earlier. His fear that someone might be inside was put to rest, however, when he found nothing and no one in the cab. He tried to start the engine but found it still wouldn't work.

As he shut the door, the four humanoids appeared in the middle of the road, as before, gesturing to one another. They went to the right side of the ship parked there and apparently entered it, just before it climbed to an altitude of about fifty feet. The same low humming sound was heard, but it stopped as soon as the UFO came to rest.

It appeared to Sanchez that the UFO was clearing the road so he could leave, just as it had done the night before. The truck started instantly this time, and the lights came on.

"And I buzzed out of there!" he told investigators.

Apparently his survival instinct was not as strong as it had been nearly twenty-four hours earlier, for he stopped the truck about six hundred feet down the road, climbed from the cab, and walked back to the area where the three UFOs were located. The one that had lifted from the highway to let him pass was once again in place on the asphalt paving.

He hid in a clump of bushes about thirty feet from the four humanoids and observed the nearest ship to see if he could find some opening in it through which the beings had been coming and going, but all he could see were unbroken walls.

He watched the beings at work. They were using

two tools that resembled a horseshoe and the letter T. They inserted the T into the ground at the embankment of the highway. Then they would withdraw the instrument and insert the horseshoe in the hole. They did not appear to be taking mineral or vegetation samples, however.

Even at close range Sanchez was not able to determine facial features on the foursome.

Not more than about three minutes passed before fear returned to Sanchez, a fear that was stronger than his curiosity. He later reported that the beings never looked in his direction or seemed aware that he was there, but he felt it was time to return to his truck and head for home.

When he reported the incident to his boss the next day, he was advised to contact the Civil Guard, which he did, accompanied by his employer's son.

The officer in charge contacted headquarters in Bejar, and after three days an officer arrived and filed a report, following an interview with Sanchez. Investigators went to the alleged landing site, where they found some strange tracks. On the highway where the craft had landed the investigators found a deep, straight groove, as if the asphalt had been scored by a very hard object. On the embankment the investigators found two scratches that seemed to substantiate Sanchez's story about the tools, but this was all the physical evidence the investigators found to indicate that the craft and its strange visitors had been there.

A few days later, two individuals from Madrid arrived in Lagunilla, stating that they were UFO investigators. They were equipped with instruments for making tests, including a Geiger counter. The team, trained in such investigative matters, was successful in finding three circles that appeared to have been caused by the craft resting there. The grass was pressed down, but no indentation from the landing gear could be found. Abnormal radioactivity in the area was recorded by the Geiger counter.

As a footnote, Sanchez added that although his truck started that night, the battery was completely dead the next morning. When he had it recharged, the garage mechanic could detect nothing abnormal about the battery.

The strange-craft sightings did not stop here, however. On March 30 Sanchez was once again with his girl friend in Pineda. It was 12:45 A.M. when they saw what looked like two large spotlights in the sky at about twenty-eight hundred feet. The spots of very bright light were flying over the area, and they gave every indication of being similar to the UFOs witnessed by him earlier that month.

The fourth and final sighting took place in early May of the same year, while Sanchez was with his girl friend and her uncle.

Sanchez had gone to the city of Salamanca, his home town, to take a driving examination for a first-class permit. It was about 6:30 A.M. when Anuncia saw a strong, white aerial light, which soon disappeared.

A few miles down the road they saw another bright light—this one coming directly toward them at an extremely high speed. Anuncia feared that it was going to strike them head on, but about three hundred feet before impact, the light changed direction, passed over their car, and disappeared.

Sanchez reported no further sightings of UFOs or humanoids, and soon after these experiences he went into the Army. While curiosity at times may have overcome fear, he was quoted in a radio interview as saying "There is no need to go on about bravery; before I did not know what fear was, but now indeed I know what it is."

TERROR IN KENTUCKY

The night of January 6, 1976, will live long in the memories of three Kentucky women who were returning home from a late supper when they were abducted by a UFO crew and put through a torturous ordeal for more than one hour.

The three women, all reportedly of the highest moral character, were Elaine Thomas, forty-eight; Louise Smith, forty-four; and thirty-five-year-old Mona Stafford. All live in or near Liberty, Kentucky. Two of the women are grandmothers, and Mrs. Stafford is the mother of a seventeen-year-old. None of the three could recall the full details of their experiences until they were placed under hypnosis by a professional hypnotist, Dr. R. Leo Sprinkle, a professor at the University of Wyoming.

It was 11:30 P.M. as the three women drove toward their homes from Stanford, Kentucky. They were about a mile west of Stanford when they noticed a large disc hurtle into view.

"It was as big as a football field!" [1] stated Mrs. Smith, who was driving the car that night. She continued her description by stating that it was metallic gray, with a glowing white dome, a row of red lights around the middle, and three or four yellow lights underneath.

The UFO first stopped ahead of them, then circled around behind their car, at which point the car suddenly accelerated to eighty-five miles an hour. The others screamed to slow down, but Mrs. Smith found that she had no control over the car. Some force then began dragging the car backward. At that point the three women lost consciousness, and remained unconscious for the next eighty minutes. The events that allegedly took place were brought out later under hypnosis.

The three women remembered vividly what had taken place during the lost eighty minutes—they were brought aboard the UFO to undergo complete physical examinations.

Elaine Thomas reported that she had been lying on her back in a long, narrow incubatorlike chamber. The humanoids looked to her like small, dark figures, which she estimated at about four feet tall. She reported that a blunt instrument was pressed hard against her chest, causing much pain, while something circled her throat.

Each time she tried to speak, she was choked. She cried softly under hypnosis as though reliving a horrible ordeal. It felt like hands pressing on her throat, and she could see shadowy figures passing around her. "They won't let me breathe—I can't get away!" she cried.

Under hypnosis Mrs. Smith said that she had been in a dark, hot place, and something had been fitted over her face. She begged the occupants to let her see, but when they did, she immediately closed her eyes, as whatever she saw was quite frightening! She could not describe the beings, however.

"Help me, Lord, please!" she cried. She told investigators that the interior of the UFO was very dark and that she was quite frightened. She pleaded with the humanoids to let her go, to let go of her arm.

She finally cried out, "I'm so weak I want to die!" Still later she asked them if she could go, and the next memory she had was that of seeing a street light.

Mona Stafford's memory was of lying on a bed in what seemed to be an operating room, with her right arm pinned down by some invisible force while three or four figures dressed in white gowns sat around her bed.

Apparently Mrs. Stafford was not as overcome as the others, but she did say that she seemed to remember being tortured, and that her eyes felt as though they were being jerked out of her head at one point. At another time, her stomach felt as though it had been blown up like a balloon. Next she reported that the humanoids were pulling at her feet, then bending them backward and twisting them. "I can't take no more!" she screamed, then lapsed into silence.

The next thing the three frightened women could remember was driving to Louise's home. They should have arrived about midnight, but they noticed the time was actually 1:30 A.M.—nearly one hour and twenty minutes were missing from their lives that night.

Louise reported that her neck hurt. When Mona examined it, she saw a strange red mark like a burn that had not blistered, about three inches long and an inch wide. Elaine's neck had the same type of mark on it.

The frightened women called a neighbor who lived next door to Louise, Lowell Lee. After hearing what they could recall of their adventure, he had the three women go into separate rooms and draw what they felt the strange UFO looked like. The three drawings looked very much alike.

Although the burn marks were gone in about two days, the three women still could not account for the time loss, nor could they recall anything from the time the car was pulled backward until they were driving near Huston eight miles from where they first saw the UFO.

Following the hypnotic sessions, they were given polygraph tests by Detective James Young of the Lexington police department. Young, in a sworn statement, said, "It is my opinion that these women actually believe they did experience an encounter."

Dr. Sprinkle stated that the three women, in his opinion, had specific impressions that indicated to them that they had been observed and handled by strange beings. He felt it would have been impossible for them to fake their reactions, and he commented that their experience during the time loss was similar to reports provided by UFO percipients who had had similar experiences.

Sheriff Bill Norris of Lincoln County, Kentucky, said that there had been a number of UFO sightings in the county that January.

In an article by Bob Pratt that appeared in the *National Enquirer* on October 10, 1976, Len Stringfield, a director of Mutual UFO Network, who investigated the whole incident, commented, "This is one of the most convincing cases on record."

The report of abduction, the memory loss, the missing time, and the shape of the UFO are all familiar to UFO investigators, for this is not an isolated episode. The three women are all known to be lifelong churchgoers with excellent reputations in their community. It is, in reality, but one more report of a physical examination of Earth humans by beings from other points in time or space.

One cannot but wonder, are we as strange to them as they are to us? Perhaps, but it is becoming apparent that while we continue to search for answers to UFOs and humanoids, they appear to have the technological advantage and so can examine us more closely—and perhaps they have fewer questions unanswered than we.

In the UFO abduction-examination story with which we are most familiar, the subject later informs UFOlogists or the communications media that he saw a vehicle on the ground and was either drawn to it, as if by hypnotic attraction, or was ushered into its interior by its occupants. The experience, though deemed by many people to be at best bizarre, at worst absurd, is nonetheless presented as a totally *physical* encounter.

For quite some time now I have been receiving accounts from men and women who claim to have been somehow taken aboard UFOs, during either an out-of-body experience or what seemed to be an unusual dream. Have these individuals been influenced by such well-known UFO encounters as the Betty and Barney Hill affair? Or are their experiences as valid as those of men and women who claim a physical interaction with UFOnauts?

Readers of this book are aware that I believe that there exists a symbiotic relationship between mankind and UFO intelligence and that the UFOs we sight are not only physical, but paraphysical—perhaps even a dimension of our own psyches. Each sighting or apparent physical interaction between mankind and "the Other," I suggest, becomes part of our collective unconscious and part of our common experience. Therefore, as we learn more about the nature of UFOs, we will also learn more about the nature of man.

It may be, then, that a large part of the UFO experience is concerned with man's essential self—his spirit, if you prefer. If it is possible that man's essence may soar free of the accepted limitations of time and space implied by his physical body and truly engage in "astral flight," "soul travel," or the more academic "out-of-body experience," then it may well be that the paraphysical aspect of man may more easily interact with that paraphysical species we commonly identify as the UFOnaut. Indeed, *all* accounts which tell of a subject having been taken aboard a UFO may be descriptions of a mental/spiritual/nonmaterial experience, rather than a physical/material one.

I have long been convinced that mankind has interacted with UFO intelligence ever since (and probably before) man straightened his spine and began to walk upright. Throughout his intellectual evolution man has described UFO encounters in terms of his contemporary understanding of the physical world and in the vernacular of his era.

Let us consider a parallel between UFOs and the legends which grew up around the Old Religion—Witchcraft—in the mid-1400s. For centuries the Christian Church officially ignored the practitioners of the ancient religion, but during the very dawn of the Age of Enlightenment, when men were seriously considering the structure of the universe, certain of the Church hierarchy suddenly became obsessed with devils and women flying through the air on broomsticks.

In his *AntiChrist and the Millennium,* E. R. Chamberlin makes an excellent point that may be analogous to the aspect of the UFO enigma under discussion in this chapter:

> Paradoxically, it was the Christian Church which, seeking with all its powers to combat the practice of satanism, gave that same practice a form. It was necessary to define witchcraft in order to combat it, and by so defining, the Church gave shape to what had been little more than folklore. Most of the elements that eventually went to make up witchcraft had long been abroad in Europe, but for centuries the Church had been content to dismiss them as mere fantasy. The legend of the woman who flew by night came in for particular scorn. "Who is such a fool that he believes that to happen in the body which is done only in the spirit?" Such sturdy com-

monsense was forced to give ground at last to a rising tide of fanaticism.

We originally defined the UFO experience in terms of science-fiction-type encounters with aliens who, as products of our imagination, act in the manner in which we would expect them to act. We structured the UFO enigma from its modern "beginning" in 1947 in an extraterrestrial, "war of the worlds" format. Is it possible that we may have been falsely interpreting as physical that "which is done only in the spirit"?

While certain readers may consider out-of-body experience (OBE) even more tenuous an object of pursuit than UFOs, a number of research laboratories are employing the most sophisticated scientific devices in a serious effort to establish OBE as a very real aspect of what it is to be human.

In a report on out-of-body research at the American Society for Psychical Research (*ASPR Newsletter,* No. 22, Summer 1974), Dr. Karlis Osis, Director of Research, wrote: "For the past two years, the ASPR Research Department has been fully engaged in exploring the question: Does the human personality survive after bodily death? . . . We have been following up our central hypothesis: That a human being has an 'ecsomatic' aspect, capable of operating independently of and away from his physical body—an aspect which might leave the body at death and continue to exist. Can one, we asked, really leave one's body temporarily (as in out-of-body experience or OBE) or permanently (as at death)?"

After a detailed review of current experimental projects, Dr. Osis summarized the ASPR work by stating: "The OBE research proved to be a difficult task, mainly because the full phenomenon is rarely produced at will. Our results are thus far consistent with the OBE hypothesis. After fully exploiting the research possibilities described above, we may indeed hope to have evidence for the ecsomatic existence of human personality."

Thousands of men and women have been provided with their own personal evidence and proof of the validity of the "ecsomatic existence of human personality." There is an enormous body of literature dealing with OBE, and numerous accounts of the phenomenon are to be found in mystical and religious traditions.

In an earlier work I expressed my opinion that spontaneous OBEs seem to fall into one of eight general categories: 1. projections while the subject sleeps; 2. projections while the subject is undergoing surgery, childbirth, tooth extraction, etc.; 3. projection at the time of accident, during which the subject receives a terrible physical jolt and seems to have his spirit literally thrown from his body; 4. projection during intense physical pain; 5. projection during illness; 6. projection during pseudo-death, wherein the subject "dies" for several moments and is subsequently revived;* 7. projection at the moment of death, when the deceased subject appears to a living percipient with whom he has an emotional link; 8. conscious out-of-body projections, in which the subject deliberately seeks to project his spirit from his body.

Now, it would appear, I must add yet another category: projection during which the subject feels that he has been taken aboard a spaceship and has interacted with an alien intelligence.

Consider this account of the kind of UFO-OBE which results in a recognition between strangers:

When I answered the door, I saw a friend and a

---

* Elizabeth Kübler-Ross and John Moody are authors who deal with this phenomenon in great depth.

stranger standing there. The newcomer had a look of shock on his face. For most of the evening he kept staring at me; I finally insisted that I know why. He said he had had a weird dream about someone he'd never met before, and he had recognized me as the man in the dream.

He said that in his dream he had been in a clearing some place with a lot of other people. They seemed to be waiting for someone or something. He did not know anyone there except me. He said that I smiled at him and made him feel calm and peaceful. He trusted me. Then everyone began to look up.

The sky was clear and star-studded except for a large circular patch directly overhead. Then he noticed that there was a large oval object blotting out the sky. As he realized this, an opening appeared in the center of the object, and a blue-white light spilled out.

He felt strange and he looked around to see how the others were reacting. Then he noticed that everyone was floating up toward the opening, one by one. He blacked out and came to in a dome-shaped room. The other people appeared to be awakening at the same time. Everyone had been placed in one of the chairs that lined the walls in three tiers. Across from them were electronic panels with flashing lights, dials, switches. In the center of the cabinets were two seats in front of what appeared to be control panels. Behind this area was a brilliant light. In the exact center of the room was a column, or pole, running through the floor and ceiling. A low railing, about three feet high, encircled the column.

He looked at the other men and women and they appeared to be as confused as he was. He felt as though someone were missing. Then everyone turned and looked toward the center of the room. There

173

stood a man in a close-fitting, one-piece, silvery spacesuit that covered his hands and feet. He wore a globe over his head that obscured his features. "Welcome aboard, friends," he said, as he reached up and removed the globe. And the stranger said that it was me!

Brad, I have now experienced this sort of thing again and again over a period of a year and a half. The shocked stranger, the stare, the same dream, down to the most minute details. After the fifth or sixth time, I began thinking, "Oh, no, not again!" I can't say how many times this has happened. I have lost track!

In discussing this dream-recognition phenomenon further with my correspondent, the following additional comments and details were produced:

One person having a dream about a future meeting with a stranger is an occurrence not at all unfamiliar in the literature of psychic phenomena. But we are speaking of a situation in which approximately a dozen men and women have experienced the same dream, identical to the smallest detail, all climaxing with the meeting of the same man. This bends the laws of chance out of all proportion. My correspondent wrote:

I had them draw a floor plan of the dome-shaped room. Allowing for differences in artistic ability, they all drew the same, identical floor plan. I then had them mark the position that they had occupied on the three tiers of seats, hoping that some of them would mark the same position. But none did. Each one had a different location in which he or she said they had been sitting.

I then asked them to describe the suit that I had been wearing. Again, the descriptions were identical.

174

Just about every detail that I could possibly think of, I asked; and they all agreed.

Here is another interesting facet: I asked each one of them *when* they had the dream, and none could remember. This puzzled some of them. Surely they could recall vaguely if it had been a week, two weeks, a month. But they had no idea whether it had been the night before or a month before. Apparently, the dreams were not normal dreams.

Upon further reflection, my correspondent decided to relate an extraordinary "dream" that he had experienced during the summer of 1959:

I was sitting in my lounge chair, reading, dozing. Yet I was tense, nervous, restless. Something seemed to be in the back of my mind that I seemed to have forgotten, but I shouldn't have.

Suddenly I looked toward the door. I knew someone was on the other side. I lay my book down, got up, went to the door, opened it a crack, and looked out.

There were two men there dressed in black. They could have been identical twins, they looked so much alike. They were dark-complexioned with Oriental eyes, but they were definitely not Orientals. Remember, this was in '59, long before you people started talking about "Men-in-Black."

They never said a word, but I heard inside my mind: "Are you ready?"

I don't know why, but for some reason or other, I was ready to go. Since it was so terribly hot that night, I had stripped down to my birthday suit, so I reached for a pair of walking shorts. Again, I heard inside my head: "That will not be necessary.

175

No one will see you." Strangely enough, that seemed to satisfy me.

We stepped out into the hall, then instantly we were on top of a flat hill in back of the apartments. I was rather surprised that the scene had changed so quickly. I noticed the headlights of a car coming down the street, and I ducked behind the two men. I didn't want to be seen running around in my birthday suit.

I heard some laughter in my mind: "We told you no one would see you. Try it!"

I boldly stepped around in front of them, spread my feet apart, propped my hands on my hips, daring anyone to see me. The car, with a man and a woman in it, passed a few feet from us. They didn't even look in my direction. It was as if we weren't there. That surprised me.

I turned to say something to my companions, and they were looking up. (This is the part of my experience that is similar to the "dreams" the strangers told me.) I followed their gaze and realized that something was hanging there suspended above us. As I did so, an opening appeared in its center, and blue-white light came tumbling out of it.

I felt a queasy sensation in the pit of my stomach, like when you are in an elevator or an airplane that is dropping too fast. I could see the apartment houses and the ground receding below us. We were floating up toward whatever that thing was. I blacked out as we were approaching the opening.

When I came to, I was lying on my side facing a wall. I rolled over on my back and sat up. I was in an oddly shaped room. The best way I know how to describe it is it was like a wedge of pie with the point of it bitten off.

The whole room was bare except for some kind

of projection on which I was sitting. Everything seemed to be made out of a blue-gray material. While the walls were very hard, the surface on which I was sitting was soft, even though everything seemed to have been made of the same material. The room was bathed in a soft glow and there were no shadows anywhere, but there was no light source that I could see.

I heard a female voice say, "He's awake now."

I looked around to see if I could spot a speaker, a TV camera, or something; but again I saw nothing but blank walls and ceiling.

About this time on the short wall—the one bitten off the end of the pie wedge—a door appeared and opened. I could see into a hallway. Although the hall was dark, there was blue-white illumination that appeared as though it was coming from some great distance.

Two shadows flittered across the doorway. I couldn't tell anything about their shapes. The movement was too rapid and too distorted.

But I got a mental impression, if you will, of two people approaching—a man in the front and a woman in the back—carrying a tray full of some kind of surgical instruments and hypodermic syringes.

The next thing I knew, I was back in my apartment, in my chair, reading my book. I gave a shudder and thought how sleepy I was. I went to bed, laughing about what a vivid imagination I have.

My correspondent said that when he awakened the next morning, he regarded the whole episode as a strange dream. But when he reached for the book he had left on his desk, he found that it had disappeared.

For two days he searched the apartment without finding the book he had been reading when the bizarre experience had interrupted him.

When my correspondent's roommate, a Special Agent of the FBI, returned from a trip, he challenged him to prove his effectiveness by finding the missing book. The two men turned the apartment upside down searching for the vanished volume.

"We started at one end of the apartment," he writes, "and we moved, dusted, waxed, and cleared everything all the way to the other end. We found things we had forgotten about, things that we'd thought we had lost some place, but no sign of the book."

Then, about one week later, the two men suddenly found the missing book on the edge of the desk, right where my correspondent had left it:

If this book did indeed vanish from our apartment and reappear, the question is *how?* Which goes back to that dream sequence again. If it really happened, how did I get back in the apartment, since when I pulled the door closed behind us, it locked automatically—and I had no key in my birthday suit!

If we assume for a moment that the dream sequence really occurred, it brings up some interesting points. For one, the possibility of teleportation. When I was led out into the hall, we were instantly on top of the hill. There was no time lapse. It was almost an instantaneous thing.

If we did teleport, why didn't we teleport directly to the UFO? The only explanation I can reason out is that somehow or other the UFO was shielded or had some kind of radiation that prevented teleportation and we had to be levitated inside.

When I dream, I usually know, even in my dream, that I am dreaming. But in this case, I didn't have that knowledge, or even that feeling, of a dream. It was dreamlike because I had so little control over my actions, but there was no sense of time lapse between the moment I was reading my book and the moment I looked up at the door. If I had nodded off to sleep in those seconds, I would assume that there would have been a feeling of change; yet there didn't seem to be any. The only change seemed to be that I suddenly lost control of myself and became more of a robot than anything else.

I think a lot of us have been controlled telepathically, somehow or other, by the UFO intelligence. That's just a feeling I have. I have no proof.

That's the trouble with the whole UFO phenomenon. What concrete evidence is there? All the weird things that have occurred around UFOs seem to be leading us more into the area of parapsychology.

For my *Gods of Aquarius: UFOs and the Transformation of Man,* Dr. Andrija Puharich and his associate Melanie Toyofuku told me of their research with the "little Uri Gellers," the "space kids," who are sprouting up all over the world with demonstrable psychokinetic abilities and extremely high IQs. Puharich mentioned that these boys and girls very straightforwardly claim to visit spaceships in their astral bodies.

"The funny thing is," Puharich said, "when two of them meet in a spaceship, they start swapping notes. It's really funny, and they're very cool about it."

Puharich told of an interesting experience that he had had in Mexico. He gathered six of the space kids and started teasing them with some equations and symbols that he told them "aren't known on Earth."

He wrote some things out and asked the kids if any of them recognized the equations.

"Yeah," said one of the kids, "but you didn't draw it right. There's a little thing that should go here!"

"Immediately the kids got into it," Puharich told me. "In one half-hour—and I have all this on tape—they'd gone through the various progressions.

"When I asked them later if they'd ever thought about these problems before, it came out that they had not. But somehow they had remembered it, either from these classes aboard spaceships or preprogramming and getting it all together!"

If these out-of-body beamings aboard UFOs are genuine spiritual experiences, what purpose do they serve?

Can it be that certain of our species are being programmed to serve as mentors and guides to others of us during the years of change and transition that lie ahead?

Are certain men and women being brought somehow into an awareness, a recognition of one another so that they can more effectively serve as "seed people" during the period that the Amerindians term the Time of Great Purification?

Or, as some more-cautious researchers might state it, is an alien intelligence programming certain of *Homo sapiens* to serve as automatons and Judas goats to lead their fellows into servitude?

I certainly do not believe the skeptical can simply laugh away all these experiences as the results of "bits of undigested beef" or the products of overactive imaginations. Whatever else these OBE-UFO dreams indicate, they certainly underscore the all-pervasive influence of the UFO as a contempoary activating archetype. There is no symbol today that affects more people on a global scale than the UFO, the "flying saucer."

CHAPTER ELEVEN

Angels in Spacesuits

For several years now I have been collecting accounts from serious-minded men and women who are convinced that they have interacted with angelic beings or, as they are nowadays frequently called, Space Brothers.

I have reports from those who maintain that they were brought food when they were starving, blankets when they were freezing, even money when they were desperately in need of funds. And these men and women are talking about actual materialization of the desired objects, not fortuitous events which brought about their acquisition.

I have accounts of those who were led to safety through fires, mountain passes, and fierce battles by the manifestation of angelic beings.

I have correspondence from those who have literally had their lives transformed in "the twinkling of an eye" through the catalyst of a personal blending with angelic intelligence.

I have beautiful testimonies from those men and women who claim lifelong supportive energy from benevolent entities who have truly served as guardian angels.

Angelic entities seem to be paraphysical, both material and nonmaterial. Although most often invisible and nonphysical, they can manifest as solidly as those men and women whose lives they seek to affect.

The Reverend Billy Graham, whose best-seller hails angels as "God's secret agents," and he larger Judeo-Christian community hardly have the monopoly on angels. My research has firmly established the universality of both a spiritual and a physical interaction between mankind and what are most often described as "light beings."

These beings have manifested in all times and in all places. There appears to be no religion that does not acknowledge their existence in firm, sometimes dogmatic, pronouncements. There is no society known to man that has not left dramatic accounts of such beings.

The manifestations of these archetypal angelic images throughout the world seems to be telling us that we are part of a larger community of intelligences, a much more complex hierarchy of powers and principalities, a potentially richer kingdom of interrelated species— both physical and nonphysical—than we have until recently been bold enough to believe. And the rewards of truly understanding the vast implication of this other intelligence are greater than we have dared to envision.

Who are angels really? Are they synonymous with UFO intelligences? Or with fairies, Wee People, and other supernatural companions?

I see angelic intelligence communicating essentially through the subconscious. That is why experiences with angels seem to happen more often, and most effectively, when the percipient is in an altered state of consciousness. That is why all UFO experiences, fairyland experiences, and angelic manifestations sound so much like dreams. They are really taking place when the percipient is in a dreamlike state. The conscious mind of the percipient remembers certain highlights of the experiences—or interprets the symbols and lessons in a consciously acceptable manner—but the actual teaching mechanism and the important mental constructs have been indelibly etched on the subconscious.

When the percipient relates his experience with a paraphysical intelligence, an astute listener often feels as though something very important has been omitted from the report, just as one often thinks a dreamer is leaving out the best parts when he retells his nocturnal adventures.

That is why we have so often used hypnosis on percipients of paraphysical phenomena—and why we ask them to recall dreams and other subconscious activities. We can thus obtain a better clue to what actually happened during the UFO experience, the fairyland adventure, the angelic manifestations, if we talk to the subconscious, rather than the conscious. The conscious is like the child who has been told only that with which he can deal intellectually, emotionally, spiritually. The wise old subconscious has a more complete picture of what the experience actually involved.

I have come to accept an objective, external, multi-dimensional reality for angelic entities, but I am prepared to concede quite readily that many instances of "angelic" communication took place with an externalized projection of the percipient's own Higher Self.

But whether an angel is an *objective-interacting* intelligence or a *subjective-interacting* intelligence, the goal of either kind of manifestation is the same: the spiritual evolution of mankind. Either manifestation is seeking to bring about the transformation of *thinking* man into *spiritual* man by urging him to realize his full potential.

SPACE BROTHERS FROM ANOTHER DIMENSION

It was on the afternoon of May 30, 1976, that Clarisa Bernhardt had that "most terrible vision." She saw native villages shaking wildly and collapsing. She sensed mud slides and the awful stench of death. She saw people running in blind panic. Clarisa instantly realized that she was having a prevision of an earthquake.

"I had the strong feeling that it was taking place on an island in the western Pacific," she recalled. "My lips were trembling as I asked myself again and again: When will this happen? Where will this happen?"

Suddenly the vision of a calendar appeared in her mind. The pages flapped open to the month of June. There was a circle around June 26.

"A few seconds later," Clarisa said, "the figure seven flashed before my eyes. I knew then that the earthquakes would be of the magnitude of seven on the Richter scale."

On May 31, Clarisa notified Dr. John Derr, geophysicist and coordinator of the U.S. National Earthquake Information Service in Denver, that there would be an earthsquake in the western Pacific on June 26 that would register 7 on the Richter scale.

Derr commented that he logged the prediction in the Service's computer, "Because we are researching the accuracy of psychics in forecasting earthquakes."

Clarisa also presented her prediction to seismologist Dr. David Stewart, director of the MacCarthy Geophysics Laboratory at the University of North Carolina.

At 4:00 A.M. on June 26, an earthquake struck the island of New Guinea. It registered 7.1 on the Richter scale.

"Mrs. Bernhardt's accuracy was remarkable," Derr stated. "It was far beyond the possibility of chance."

"I'm convinced psychics can predict earthquakes," Stewart commented. "Clarisa Bernhardt has proved that. Current technology could not have achieved anywhere near the accuracy she accomplished. The best science could have done in predicting this particular earthquake would have been to forecast that it would occur sometime within a period of six to eight months."

"The vast majority of psychics are whistling in the dark," Derr said, "but Clarisa has had some damn close hits that are hard to ignore."

Clarisa's series of "hits" began in November 1974, when she predicted a 3:00 P.M. Thanksgiving Day quake in Hollister, California, that would register 5.2 on the Richter scale. She was off by one minute: The tremors began at 3:01 P.M., Thursday, November 28.

In addition to the 1974 central California quake, Clarisa is credited with accurately predicting the dates, locations, and magnitudes of the two largest quakes felt on this planet in 1975—the 7.8 quake of May 26 in the Azores (she missed this by only two hours and eleven minutes); and the 7.2 quake of November 29 in the Hawaiian Islands (this one was exactly on target).

Since her visit to the MacCarthy Geophysics Laboratory in North Carolina on January 5, 1976, Clarisa has been attempting to interpret her psychic impressions of earthquakes to comply with more rigid scientific criteria. It is her earnest desire to be of greater practical service to scientists working in this field, so now when she makes an earthquake prediction she has the information notarized and immediately mailed to various scientific groups. At the U.S. Geological Survey in Denver, her predictions are fed into a computer, which will give a readout sometime after the calendar date of the occurrence.

Clarisa is one psychic who does not enjoy being accurate. The realization of such prognostications as the New Guinea quake is very heartbreaking for the attractive blonde seeress. "Someday psychics and scientists must work out an ultra-warning/ultra-evacuation system so that lives need not be lost in terrible catastrophes," she said.

It is Clarisa's great concern for human life that compelled her to notify the FBI about the chilling psychic vision she experienced on August 5, 1975, in which she saw "Red Riding Hood" aiming a pistol at President Gerald Ford. She impressed the fact on her contact with the federal investigative branch that President Ford would be in danger from a female assassin who would be wearing a red-hooded cape. The confrontation would take place, she said, in Sacramento, California, on September 5, 1975.

Was it because of Clarisa's warning that Presidential bodyguards were so readily able to thwart the actions of the red-hooded Lynette (Squeaky) Fromme?

It is also a matter of record that Clarisa predicted, well in advance of the actual occurrence, the exact date and place (September 18, 1975, in San Francisco) that Patty Hearst would be apprehended. On her *Exploration* radio program, Clarisa physically foresaw grave danger for King Faisal of Saudi Arabia during Easter Week of 1975. She feels that the King Faisal prediction went "unprevented" because she was then comparatively unknown, and no one in authority took her seriously.

Now Clarisa is regularly and seriously consulted by

both local and federal law-enforcement agencies. "I hope that every prediction I ever make about assassination or murder will be prevented," she said firmly. "I never want to be accurate in this regard. I want the authorities to be able to apprehend the murderers ahead of the event and prevent my predictions from coming to pass!"

Dr. Telemachos Grennias, a clinical psychologist investigating paranormal phenomena for the Episcopal Archdiocese of Northern California, stated: "Clarisa has made private predictions for me, and her accuracy rate is amazingly high. I am convinced that events will prove her to be without equal anywhere in the world. I believe she will prove to be the most important psychic yet discovered."

And to what source does Clarisa credit her remarkable foreknowledge of events?

During a series of discussions with Clarisa and her husband, Russ, while we were attending to our respective speaking engagements in Oklahoma City in June 1976, I learned that she was convinced that she had experienced an encounter with alien entities.

Clarisa: On two or three occasions they have "transported" me. I am not going to say physically because at this time my body was still on the bed. But they took my consciousness aboard the spaceship. I felt very humble about getting to go there, so I just listened. At the time, they gave me some predictions, but they felt since I was sensitive toward earthquakes the scientists and so forth would be more impressed if I gave them the two largest earthquakes of that year.

There were three of the gentlemen, and they were about five eight to five ten in height. They had on silver-colored uniforms. These gentlemen had helmets on, so I wasn't able to see the details of their faces. But I did not feel that their heads were out of proportion with their bodies. In other words, they did not present a grotesque appearance as far as our human understandings are concerned.

When I asked them who they were, they told me that I might think of them as Space Brothers. A lot of their people have been in suspended animation, and they said that our people on this particular planet will learn more about that in the near future. They gave me the name of their world, but it was very unpronounceable as far as I was concerned. They said that they had come from several galaxies away. Sometimes they travel back and forth in time, as well as in space.

They told me that they were very concerned about some of the things that have been happening here on Earth. They're afraid that we are going to have problems with nuclear power. If we blow ourselves up, it's going to mess up some things in the universe.

They are here on a peaceful mission—a mission of peace and love. They would like to communicate with everyone. There will be more contact, but for the most part, they feel that man has only evolved above certain primitive emotional characteristics.

They emphasized to me that thoughts are things. Every man on this planet has the responsibility to learn to control his thoughts and to direct them in a positive manner. As soon as we can do that, they will appear physically in many areas.

Can you recall the physical description of the interior of the craft?

Clarisa: One particular area to which they took me was as big as a city block. They took me into an area where crew members were sleeping. There were rows of six as far back as I could see.

Did they speak verbally or mentally in the communication area?

Clarisa: They spoke to me mentally, because each time they contacted me there was this light that came forth. It was as if I were hearing them this way.

Was the sound a mechanical one, a "human" sound, a computerlike sound? Did you hear it in your voice or their voice?

Clarisa: It was in English, and it was not a computerlike sound. There was strength behind it. There was no doubt when they told me something.

What do you think their purpose is in giving you the information about the earthquakes?

Clarisa: They said they wanted to assist me. They knew that I was trying to help people. Although I have this ability through my own development (they said my metaphysical studies had made me more sensitive), I was a clear receiver when they had a reason to contact me.

Did they give any indication as to how long they had been aware of life on Earth? Do you feel their presence is a recent thing or that they have been around for a long time?

Clarisa: From what I understood, it's as if they have been waiting for the people on Earth to grow up. This is the best way I know how to express it.

I do definitely feel from my contact with them that they are going to come here and intercede. I don't mean they are going to come in and start fighting with people. But because of their abilities, they have a lot of knowledge which can help us.

Do they make reference to a Supreme God force throughout the universe?

Clarisa: They did not make any reference to this. I let them talk to me, and I asked a minimum of questions. I feel that they are a higher and more evolved form of life than we are at this point. I'm sure there are more things in the universe to behold than our present consciousness can understand.

Did they give any indication as to any other projects that they might be encouraging?

Clarisa: The main area in which they want to help our Earth is in the advancement of scientific avenues. If we can prove ourselves worthy, they would like very much to have us in a position whereby we might communicate and learn a whole lot about the universe.

Following the above interview, a telephone call was placed to Dean Sterling, Ph.D., Executive Director of the Institute of Psi Research and Development in Oklahoma City, and another interview was arranged.

The Institute of Psi Research and Development is the experimental and training arm of Psi Seven, a corporation dedicated to the investigation of all areas of psychic phenomena and the dissemination of this information to the general public.

After talking with the Bernhardts, Dr. Sterling, a hypnologist and hypnophysiologist, hypnotized Clarisa and taped the following testimony:

Dr. Sterling: What happened on your way to San Jose? What was the first thing that happened that was strange to you after you left your house that day?

Clarisa: I am late. I now see there's not much traffic. I'm not going to be late. But I feel funny. I feel dizzy. There's no reason for it. It's getting stronger now.

What's getting stronger?

Clarisa: The strange feeling I have in my fore-head. It's coming all over me. I feel awful. I feel like I'm falling out of my body. I have to drive the car! I hope I don't faint.

How fast are you driving?

Clarisa: I'm driving fifty-five. I'm going to slow down, because I'm concerned I might have an accident or go off the road. But there is something that I can't explain. It's like it's in my forehead. Hurts my head. Something's happening. Voices are saying something.

What are the voices saying?

Clarisa: [*Beginning to get upset*] They're telling me, "Don't be afraid." I don't know if I'm dying or what. Wait . . . Wait . . . But they're telling me I'm not to talk.

I hear a man's voice. He says his name is Marisha. He says, "Don't be afraid." But I am afraid. [*Crying*] I cannot explain what's happening. I'm not driving my car. It's like there's a cloud over the car. I think I'm gonna faint.

What type of cloud?

Clarisa: It's like a mist. It's like a big thing coming around the car. I don't know what it is. Good God . . . They said not to be afraid. Wait! What's happening now? There's five . . . figures in front of me.

What do you see around you?

Clarisa: I can't . . . I am *hearing* something. "Don't be afraid." There's one coming forward. He's not speaking. But it's coming into my mind. He says his name is Marisha. "We are from another time and from another light. You will understand that we came not to hurt you. We must explain things to you."

Explain your surroundings. Can you see what's around you?

Clarisa: It's like we're in a building. It's circular.

It's like we're in a circle, and there's a lot of equipment in here. The car is here. It's like we're in a big garage, except there's no window. It's like it's a very sterile place.

What are they telling you?

Clarisa: They're telling me that I will think of them as Space Brothers. They come only to communicate with me. They're sorry if they frightened me. I feel better. I feel that there's not as much to be afraid of now. I think I'm understanding now. Two of them are coming forward.

There are some lights around the room. Looks like a lot of instruments. I think it's similar to the panel of an airplane . . . the controls. A computer. There's lots of information, and there are things happening on it.

What are the Space Brothers saying?

Clarisa: They tell me that I will learn more about them. They're sorry they had to frighten me, but it was necessary to show me that they had control. I must never doubt that they have control over me or anyone else. They do not ordinarily do this, but they said that it was important that I understand. They will be in contact with me in a few days.

Why are they in control of you? Why have they chosen to be in control of you?

Clarisa: They tell me that the reason they are in control of me is that they can control anyone. This is not their way of getting people to do things, but they wanted to impress me with the fact that it can be done. They say to me that because of the position I am in because of my radio show, they feel I can do much to further their mission.

They come in peace. They do not want to hurt anyone. But they do worry about us.

They say that mankind is on the verge of making a mess out of things. If we wish to destroy ourselves it is fine, but there is a responsibility to the universe. For this reason I can be of help to them by making others more aware that there are others in this universe besides those of us here on this planet. They say that we have not been responsible and that we have much growing to do.

They are not caught in time, as we are caught in time. We will learn of this in the future.

They told me that they would let me return and that I would then be conscious of my experience.

They told me that they would contact me more in the future. And that I would not be frightened of them.

I was very interested in what was inside the ship because it looked so big. There was a very interesting checkered floor pattern.

They told me that I would have confusion, but it would clear up. I must be impressed with the fact that they can control many people, but they do not wish to do this. I am concerned that they do not have feelings of compassion.

Why are you concerned that they don't have compassion?

Clarisa: They are good, but they are so cold . . . I have a feeling that . . . they have a different understanding of life from ours. Perhaps it is because they have so much knowledge.

I think I am going to be able to leave and go back now.

Before you go, do they give you any formulas or any new scientific knowledge that would help us?

Clarisa: There is a formula for fuel.

Try to tell me what it is.

Clarisa: I see the first letters. There's a Y. There's an R. There's a loop number . . .

What number?

Clarisa: It's like a two. There is a Z. A funny-looking slash like a check mark. There is another number that is like an H. Then there is a letter T and RHC. There's a two again; an H; then there's a O, P, Y. All of this is underscored. And over this . . . there's an R two Y and V.

This is all I can see at this time. They said that this formula would be important. This is what would help people in the fuel problems. It could be that it must be handled in the proper way because it has something to do . . . they told the words . . . I cannot recall them all. I want to say two words. One is like "plutonium" and another is like "lithium." There is a connection between the two things. I'm confused about this.

There is a strange glow in here, and I think I'm told that I'm going back. They said they send only thoughts of love.

I'm starting to get dizzy again . . . but I'm not going to be frightened this time. I do believe them. There is a glow. It's like a fire. Then there's this mist, like a cloud, that's happening again.

They said that I may not remember for a little bit, but I will remember later on in the day. I will be contacted again. They will be with me, yet they will not be with me, for the next few days and the next few hours.

I'm getting dizzy, and my ears are ringing. There's this hurting again. And I feel like my head's gonna pop. But I'm not going to be frightened. I just breathe deeper.

What's happening? I must have fainted! I don't know where I am.

Where are you?

Clarisa: This is weird. In San Jose!

Where in San Jose!

Clarisa: I don't know where I am. I have to drive down here to the road and look at the sign because . . .

San Jose is back the other way. It says Oakland is ahead. My God . . . How did I get here?

Today, secure in the knowledge that her channeled information has been of genuine value, Clarisa Bernhardt declares that she is here to advise people. "I do not make things up," she emphasizes. "It is as if I see things that are going to happen appear on a movie screen.

"I'm not trying to project gloom, but, rather, I want to get people aware of certain things so we can establish preventive measures."

Clarisa foresees that, beginning in March 1978, the West Coast will change its physical configuration enormously. San Diego will become an island. South of Santa Barbara, the land mass will be converted into a chain of islands.

"I do not see a great loss of life, however," the seeress commented. "The tremors and the shifts and changes will be gradual enough to permit evacuation of the areas affected.

"Yes, the poles will shift . . . but very gradually . . . no sudden slips. And the new polar alignment will be more harmonious for the Earth.

"The Imperial Valley will go back into the sea. A new bay will open up, and there will be a waterway clear up to Arizona."

Clarisa has been given an "8" in conjunction with this prediction, which causes her to state that the dramatic alteration of the Pacific Coast will begin on

March 8, 1978. The period of seismic trauma and turmoil will span ten years.

San Francisco Bay will become an inland sea. Los Angeles, as well as San Diego, will be transformed into offshore islands of a new continent that will have risen from the floor of the Pacific.

"And Phoenix," she stated firmly, "will be known as the Port City of the West. A beautiful rivicra, a marvelous marina will stretch across the southwestern United States."

Whether Clarisa's source is Space Brothers or intuitive levels of her own higher consciousness, we do not have long to await our own personal appraisal of her predictions.

The concept of benign humanoid entities from other worlds visiting Earth did not really become a part of contemporary man's popular mythology until George Adamski claimed to have contacted a Venusian flying-saucer pilot near Desert Center, California, on November 20, 1952. Adamski communicated with the UFO-naut through telepathic transfer, with such great success that the contactee was able to produce two best-sellers in his lifetime (*Flying Saucers Have Landed* and *Inside the Space Ships*) and become an even more highly controversial figure after his death than he was during his peak years as a missionary of the Space Brothers' gospel. To those who have made a cult of the flying saucer, Adamski is revered as our first ambassador to outer space. To the skeptical, Adaski epitomizes the kookiness and crackpotism that swirls around UFO research. To the researcher who takes himself "seriously," Adamski personifies the stigma which keeps the orthodox scientist from becoming involved in an open pursuit of the UFO enigma.

Louis Cassels, religion writer for United Press International, commented in an August 1969 press story that those who believe the Earth to be unique in all creation as the abode of life might find the discovery of alien life on other planets a most shattering experience if they have "entered the space age with a stone-age conception of God." Cassels continues:

> If, for example, a man believes in God solely because he feels this hypothesis is necessary to explain the emergence of life on earth, he would surely be disconcerted by evidence that the same "miracle" has occurred elsewhere. But there is really no need for any Christian or Jew to pin his religious faith to the precarious proposition that earth is the only place where the creative will of God has been expressed in the bringing forth of life.

The Reverend G. H. Nicholson, rector of the Church of St. Mary the Virgin, Burfield, England, published his astonishingly unorthodox views on UFOs in an issue of the Church's regular newsletter. Nicholson begins by discussing the global range of the UFO phenomena and poses the question of whether these things be the "chariots of God" mentioned in the Scriptures or if they might be the instruments of a "Satanically indwelt person on Earth." The rector next displays his awareness of the contactees' basic message: The Space Brothers are messengers of God; their present task is to monitor the Earth and assist the Judgment Day that will soon be upon man; they will be responsible for a mass "space-lift" of all of God's true followers and for the caring of these good people on another world while the Earth is cleansed in a crucible of fire and destruction. After cautioning all Christians against the fearful Satanic Deception that will seek to delude the entire world in the last days and admonishing all good people to test the Space Brothers against the exhortations in Scripture, Nicholson reminds his flock:

Jesus has shown us that the heavens are inhabited by His angels and His elect, and that when He returns, His angels will "gather together His elect from the four winds and from one end of heaven to the other."

St. Paul declares that the faithful living at the time of the Judgment "will be caught up together with them in the clouds to meet the Lord in the air."

A prophecy in Psalms tells of the sphere vehicles in this event. "The chariots of God are twenty thousand, even thousands of angels; the Lord is among them."

A passage in Isaiah speaks of the joy that will be experienced on earth when it has been cleansed of all evil . . . "For behold the Lord will come with fire, and with his chariots like a whirlwind to render his anger with fury, and his rebuke with flames of fire."

Nicholson concludes his affirmation of belief in the reality of the UFO phenomenon and its possible association with certain of the prophecies in Scripture by saying: "If the saucers should cause us to believe in God and His word; to repent of our national and individual sins, and to turn to Him with all of our heart in view of what surely shall come to pass, they will have served a very great purpose, in addition to any role they may have to play in the days to come."

Lord Soper, Britain's outspoken Methodist peer,

stated publicly his view that sentient beings could exist in the universe who have none of the physical sense of man: "They could exist as a mass of radio waves, or something equally strange to us who are so used to thinking in anthropomorphic terms."

The clergyman saw no reason to question one's faith in God if beings from space should ever visit Earth. "If there is intelligent life on a star like Epsilon Eridani, or on planets circling it, these beings must have their own incarnation of God," Lord Soper said. "This fact should not invalidate at all the picture we have of God in Jesus Christ. Christ is the human photograph of God, but beings on other worlds must have their own appropriate photographs of the Eternal Spirit."

Father Lambert Dolphin, research physicist at California's Stanford Research Institute, has been quoted in the press as declaring: "The mounting evidence leads me to believe that UFOs are extraterrestrial in origin, piloted by intelligent beings. Their appearance in recent years is probably in some way associated with the imminent second coming of Jesus Christ."

Rabbi Norman Lamm, Jewish theologian, has issued his opinion that no basic tenet of Judaism would be threatened by the scientific discovery that man is "not the only intelligent and biospiritual resident of God's world." Although the Bible emphasizes the unique nature of man, Rabbi Lamm points out, such a teaching is not an assertion that the remainder of the universe lacks intelligent life. Such a doctrine simply affirms "the spiritual dignity of creatures endowed with reason and free will."

The Jewish theologian states that on Earth only man fulfills these unique conditions, but "if we should discover other free and rational species, we shall, of course, include them in the community of uniquely biospiritual creatures."

In *Gods of Aquarius,* I include the account of Francie, the New Age mystic and contactee, who related how, during her first meeting with angelic entities, the principal communicator spoke in a strange singsong manner.

Francie: Dad began pounding the nail into the wall behind me to my right. The curtains were sheer and blowing, and it was spring. The window was to my left and open, and the curtains were flapping and almost touching my legs. I remember all this very vividly, though I was only five. Perhaps *they* have seen to it that I have.

To my right and above me, I became aware of a person coming slowly down, right through the ceiling. He alighted so gently that he stood almost directly before me, and I wasn't certain if he ever touched the floor. His white robe was draped over one shoulder, and the wind made it flow in and out around his body. His hair was straw-colored and straight, and was styled in a page-boy cut coming down to the base of his neck. His eyes were blue, wide-set. He had a large, full jaw and fair skin. There appeared to be no beard-growth area. I remember because my dad often had a five-o'clock-shadow-type growth . . .

. . . I don't know why I have thought all these years that he was an angel unless that entity placed the knowledge of who he was, and what an angel was, into my mind without my knowing it. He began to speak, but his voice kept rising and falling in tone, as one would sing and talk at the same time.

I interrupted him and yelled to my dad, "Dad, look! There's an angel in the room!" I turned to see if Dad were looking. His back was facing me, and his hand was held high in the midst of striking a nail. He was motionless. I pleaded for him to please look, and then I noticed another angel in the upper corner of the room, just to the left of Dad's head.

I said, "If you won't turn around, just look at the one by your head." But Dad did not move. The angel above his head was a woman. Only her face and hair were visible to me. She looked as if she were from a different place from the male angel, as she had darker skin, eyes, and hair. Her dark hair was quite wavy and hung past her small-featured face.

My angel, the male, continued to sing-talk, and I remembered several phrases for years, though they made no sense to me. I shouted to my mother and saw another female face in the right corner wall that was in front of me. I then glanced at all the corners, two remaining, and there were four angels in total. . . .

. . . I called for my mother to come quickly, that there were angels in the room. Upon doing so, the male angel totally changed his voice. No longer was it a gentle, high-pitched singing one, but a low, harsh monotone, [a] mechanical voice. He said, "Do not tell your parents."

Mother responded that she was busy washing dishes, and the angel continued to sing-talk some more until he and the women faded away.

Dad resumed pounding. . . .

. . . I know there is much more information that is locked in too tight for me to remember consciously, though it may be coming into my memory like little time-release capsules. I've often wondered, though, why such a profound mission was received by a five-year-old. They would certainly know that

I could not retain it all consciously. If it was truly to affect my life on a subconscious level, why did the angel need to appear physically? He could merely have sent it telepathically.

A few years ago, a Sheffield, England, newspaper published the results of an evening with Phillip Rodgers in his cottage on Sir William Hill in Grindleford. In addition to a number of journalists, there were engineers, scientists, and officials of astronomical societies in attendance. All those present heard weird voices, which Philip Rodgers had tape-recorded, speaking in sharply clipped accents. The voices claimed to be personages from "outer space."

Phillip Rodgers is a brilliant musician and is ranked as one of Europe's foremost artists on the recorder (woodwind, not tape!). When he is not giving lectures and concerts, he is at his tape recorder, attempting to capture sounds and voices which allegedly emanate from spaceships or people in other worlds.

Whether Rodgers's tape recorder is truly picking up alien greetings or the musician has mediumistic talents which somehow impress the sensitive tapes with ghostly sounds, the voices may indeed be said to be "unearthly." During a lengthy correspondence with me, Rodgers consented to tell the full story of his adventures with "voices from space."

In October, 1956, I had the strong hunch to walk up to the top of Sir William Hill, a long, straight, moorland road, climbing to an altitude of 1400 feet, overlooking the Derwent Valley and my own village of Grindleford, Derbyshire [England], some ten miles from the large industrial city of Sheffield. On my way down, I was rewarded by seeing a slowly pulsating light, which could not be explained. And a few weeks later, when walking down the same hill, I was "buzzed" by a brilliant object which hovered straight in front of me, switching over from white to red, then disappearing. These two experiences convinced me not only that flying saucers existed but that the intelligences behind them knew quite a bit about me. Moreover these sightings were personal ones, for my own benefit.

During the summer of the following year [1957], there were many sightings in the Sheffield area. And in September I heard a large number of musical notes, apparently produced by invisible flying objects. At other times they played scraps of melody, somewhat unrhythmic but with beautiful bell-like tone. Being a musician, I could identify them by the notes they produced. And once, while [I was] playing a recorder solo in the key of C, before an audience of three hundred schoolchildren, one of these objects, steadily emitting a note of C sharp, was heard, not only by myself, but by my fellow artists, and several members of the teaching staff. Later I heard of some people in County Rosscommon [Republic of Ireland] hearing similar sounds. So they were *not* noises in my head.

On November 24, 1957, I had the idea of recording these sounds. Placing the microphone of my Grundig machine on the outer sill of my sitting-room window, I switched on, ran downstairs, and stood in front of our gate. After a couple of minutes, I was rewarded with a peculiar, penetrating, whistling sound, apparently coming from behind the ash tree on the opposite side of our lane. Immediately I ran indoors and wound back the tape, fully expecting there to be nothing on it. But to my intense relief, there was the sound, as clear as a bell. I noticed a peculiar, rising, double fundamental note, quite alien to any sound I had heard on earth. That was my first recording of a sound believed to emanate from outer space.

Over the Christmas holiday I picked up several sounds which were hard to explain but provided no definite evidence. And it was not until February, 1958, after a very severe blizzard, that a real breakthrough occurred. I recorded several musical, dulcimerlike bleeping sounds, in between which appeared the voice of a small girl shouting: "Howdy!" a form of greeting never used in this country. This points to the possibility that, whoever the young lady was, she had learned her English in the western part of the United States.

The next breakthrough occurred on March 21st 'round about mid-day: A mechanically produced (computer) voice, saying, faintly but clearly and definitely: "Ship is real: People," against a background of clicking, resembling the noise of a typewriter. This was the first of the very few terse messages I have received. I took it to mean that the space ships are real and are piloted by people.

I must, however, correct an impression that this message was received over the radio. It was picked up through a "Golden Voice" microphone, placed outside my bedroom window, some twelve feet from the ground. My radio was not on at the time. Like nearly all my signals, however, it was not heard at the moment of reception but discovered only when I played back the tape.

Shortly after this, when recording at night, I picked up a fantastic series of musical signals, mostly of instruments unknown on earth. In particular, they seemed very keen on demonstrating the tuning. One appeared to be a violinlike instrument, tuned in fifths, but with no G string and in its place an upper

B, a fifth above the top E of a terrestrial violin. In between playing they kept shouting greetings. There was also a strange harplike instrument, improvising on strings, tuned to a somewhat modernistic chord.

A careful check revealed that broadcast performances at the time had no connection with these signals.

I must interpolate here and say that most of my recordings are fragmentary, many of them only a second or two in duration. There are no messages from "The Master of Venus" to the erring people of Earth, exhorting men to live together in brotherhood, to abolish war, the H-Bomb, etc. Many of my signals are meaningless on their own. But, if fitted together like pieces of a jigsaw puzzle, they provide a living sound picture of the people who produces them. I have heard it said that the space people have no wish to spoon feed us. Rather, they prefer to give us scraps of evidence, like the isolated clues in a detective mystery, upon which we are able to work.

A major recording was obtained on Maunday Thursday, 'round about 8:45 P.M. Later I checked that no children had been playing in the field opposite our house. But on the tape are to be heard the voices of youngsters making animal noises, chatting, playing, and laughing among themselves, and blowing an unidentified trumpetlike instrument, playing a modernistic musical phrase, quite unlike any fanfare I have heard on earth.

A small boy who is able to speak perfect English, says; "Sputnik!" followed by what appears to be a translation into his own language: "Ya-du pardu!" And a girl of ten or eleven (Earth years!) says softly: "Halleluya!" followed by the word: "Nyanna-podo!" quietly and with Italian clarity.

A couple of weeks after the "Children's party" recording, I picked up the voice of a boy shouting: "Ya-ba hueseta!" (the "ue" as in the French "lune"). Then there is one of a very amorous young lady, saying "Mee-see-mar!" a less intimate, though still friendly greeting. The syllable: "Nya" (as in "piano") occurs in three words recorded. In addition to: "Nyanna-podo!" we have: "Nyanna-puisee!" and: "Ya-va-nyanna-donnova!"

Early one morning in Gridleford, I recorded the voice of a man, apparently speaking a different language. The word he said was: "Hiroshidoo!" And about three months later, when in Shrewsbury (Shropshire), about eighty miles away, came the voice of possibly the same man saying "Herashidu-check!" Apparently the change of vowel altered the meaning of the word. Note the subtlety of these messages. And on another occasion, a group of boys and girls shouted: "Driota" followed by a feminine giggle. About half-a-minute later, the same word was repeated, only shouted much louder. And there are several more words on my tapes.

When I look back on Easter, 1958, it seems almost like a dream, had I not several very remarkable recordings to show for it. Almost every time I switched on that machine, something very exciting came on to the tape. The high spot occurred on the Tuesday. A friend invited me to tea in Sheffield. But immediately I had the strong hunch to return home, feeling certain that some important recording had been planned, and I arrived home earlier than expected.

I switched on the machine and gave a time check. However, I made a mistake and did not use the twenty-four-hour clock, which had been my custom. On playing back the tape later that night, I was amazed to find a man's voice, rather nasal but friendly and humorous, making a somewhat hesitant correction to my time check, according to the twenty-four-hour clock, then asking if he was right. My voice is heard through the closed window and his is just as loud and clear. It appears he knew I was about to give the wrong time check and was ready with his correction, thus demonstrating the telepathic power of these people, as mentioned by so many space contactees. There is a peculiar triple click at the beginning of the recording, followed by an unearthly whirring sound. Several checks have been made since this happened and hoax [has been] entirely ruled out.

A couple of days later I tried a recording at about 4:15 A.M. in our dining room, with the machine on the table and the microphone a couple of feet in front of me. All I heard during the recording was the hum of a motor, amplified by its being on the solid oak table. But on playing back the tape, there was the sound of people, scuttling through a room with metal walls and a sliding door closing after them. There was also a sound like an air valve. And although no words were spoken, there appears to have been a girl, standing by the door, whilst a man is pushing a large object through it in a great hurry.

What I recorded is, of course, anybody's guess. Poltergeists have been suggested, but we have never had any such thing in our house. Besides, I would have heard it at the time of the recording. My guess is that the sound came from inside a space ship and that the transmitter, used for my recordings, was being pushed out through an air lock. Fanciful? Yes. But I stick to it till someone thinks of a better explanation.

A UFO investigator, who heard my "Time

Check," suggested I try recording away from home. At first I did not wish to do this, for fear of upsetting the arrangements of those responsible for the recordings. I imagined they had their apparatus pretty well set up, aiming at my bedroom window. However, I succumbed and took my machine to the home of a friend in Sheffield. Her house was on a hill, overlooking a valley about five miles wide, with the district of Firth Park on the opposite side. And I must explain that, apart from my friend, nobody in the district knew me at all. Once again I was lucky in picking up some remarkable signals, including the voice of an exceedingly feminine young lady, with a delightful giggle. In this fragment is to be heard the voice of a man saying: "Tape recorder on" and the young lady remarks: "Oh dear! It's that Rodgers come visiting." Her laugh which follows is one of the most beautiful sounds I have ever heard.

Although the reader cannot possibly form a true judgment of my recordings without having heard them, I am sure he will agree that these form a vivid picture of a people, like ourselves, men, women, and children, exceedingly friendly, jolly, and informal, yet perfectly self-disciplined, as I found to my regret when playing music. They kept perfectly quiet during a performance, making comments only before or after a piece. And yet these delightful people are completely alien to this planet, having a language and an astonishing technology completely unknown to us. I am convinced they do not live on the ground, and it is highly unlikely they come from under the earth. And although my full name has been mentioned on several occasions, only three times out of hundreds of recordings received have their names been mentioned and never their place (or planet) of origin. Nevertheless they have several times used the words: "In space!" or "From space!" and I personally regard this as a plain statement of fact.

As human beings we seem to be so very quick at judging others by ourselves. We cannot help speculating what our motives might be for carefully surveying, observing, analyzing, and evaluating an alien culture.

Invasion . . . Domination . . . Territorial Acquisition . . . Commercial Exploitation.

Check all of the above?

It would seem that if a war of the worlds had been in the game plan of the UFOnauts, we would have had a very unpleasant confrontation ages ago. Paranoid mutterings about their waiting for the proper time to mash us would seem to carry little weight as a serious argument when one considers that *Homo sapiens* surely would have been much easier to conquer and subjugate when he was hurling rocks than when he was launching nuclear weapons.

Whatever the reason for the UFOnauts' concern for planet Earth, there seems no mistaking their constant attention toward us and our environment. Whether they be time travelers avidly pursuing their history lessons, Space Brothers on a spiritual mission, or anthropologists from some distant galaxy preparing the definitive study of Earthlings, the UFOnauts appear intensely interested in the most mundane aspects of life on our planet. The evidence seems clearly to indicate that they have always been with us and that they are currently accelerating their program of interaction. But it must remain for each reader to assess what for him will be the most logical motive for such persistent reconnaissance from those beings who may well be our cosmic cousins.

BIBLIOGRAPHY AND NOTES

In addition to the author's own files and works, the principal references used in this book came from a number of excellent publications which have devoted many years to an extensive reportage of the UFO and the UFOnaut enigma.

Saga Magazine and *UFO Report*. Gambi Publications, Inc., 333 Johnson Avenue, Brooklyn, NY 11206. Under the editorial direction of Martin Singer, *Saga* has covered the UFO scene for more than a decade. Singer has recently undertaken editorial duties for *UFO Report* and increased its frequency of publication, making it a bimonthly.

Skylook (recently changed to *The Mufon UFO Journal*) is published at 103 Oldtowne Road, Sequin, TX 78155. This journal is the official publication of the Mutual UFO Network, Inc. (formerly the Midwest UFO Network).

Canadian UFO Report. PO Box 758, Duncan, B.C., Canada. Although published in Canada, this journal presents worldwide reports.

Flying Saucer Review. Compendium Books, 281 Camden High Street, London NW 1, Great Britain. A fine magazine, and perhaps the oldest regularly published journal in the field of UFOlogy.

The Ohio UFO Reporter. Route 3, Yankee Road, Middletown, OH 45042.

The Ohio Skywatcher. 5852 East River Road, Fairfield, Ohio 45014.

Official UFO. Countrywide Publications, 247 Park Avenue South, New York, NY 10010. *Ancient Astronauts* is also published at this above address.

International UFO Reporter, 924 Chicago Avenue, Evanston, IL 60202.

Saucer News is no longer published, but *Gray Barker's Newsletter* is still published at Saucerian Press, Box 2228, Clarksburg WV 26301.

CHAPTER FOUR

1. Sergio Conti, *Flying Saucer Review,* September–October 1970.
2. *Flying Saucer Review,* January–February 1969.
3. *Flying Saucer Review,* September–October 1970.
4. *Skylook,* March 1976.
5. *Skylook,* August 1975.
6. Robert A. Schmidt, *Flying Saucer Review,* September–October 1968.
7. *Canadian UFO Report,* Summer 1976.
8. *Gray Barker's Newsletter,* March 1976.

CHAPTER FIVE

1. *Ohio UFO Reporter,* March 1973.
2. Ted Bloecher, "UFO Repair Reported," *Skylook,* July 1975.
3. *Skylook,* July 1975.

CHAPTER SIX

1. *Skylook,* December 1973.

CHAPTER SEVEN

1. *Canadian UFO Report,* Vol. 3, No. 4, 1975.

2. Joan Whritenour and Brad Steiger, *Saga,* February 1968.
3. *Canadian UFO Report,* Vol. 2, No. 6, 1973.
4. Stan Gordon, "UFO and Creature Observed in Same Area in Pennsylvania," *Skylook,* June 1975.
5. Ted Bloecher, "Occupant Case Detailed," *Skylook,* November 1974.

CHAPTER TEN

1. *National Enquirer,* October 19, 1976.